Isaiah
Part Two

Isaiah
Part Two

Isaiah 40–66

Leslie J. Hoppe
with Little Rock Scripture Study staff

LITURGICAL PRESS
Collegeville, Minnesota

www.littlerockscripture.org

Nihil obstat for the commentary text by Leslie J. Hoppe: Robert C. Harren, *Censor deputatus*.
Imprimatur for the commentary text by Leslie J. Hoppe: ✝ John F. Kinney, J.C.D., D.D., Bishop of Saint Cloud, Minnesota, May 11, 2012.

Cover design by John Vineyard. Interior art by Ned Bustard. Maps on pages 11 and 12 created by Robert Cronan of Lucidity Information Design, LLC. Photos and illustrations on pages 21, 23, 37, and 51 courtesy of Getty Images.

Scripture texts in this work are taken from the *New American Bible, revised edition* © 2010, 1991, 1986, 1970 Confraternity of Christian Doctrine, Washington, D.C. and are used by permission of the copyright owner. All Rights Reserved. No part of the New American Bible may be reproduced in any form without permission in writing from the copyright owner.

 This symbol indicates material that was created by Little Rock Scripture Study to supplement the biblical text and commentary. Some of these inserts first appeared in the *Little Rock Catholic Study Bible*; others were created specifically for this book by Michael DiMassa.

Commentary by Leslie J. Hoppe, © 2012, 2023 by Order of Saint Benedict, Collegeville, Minnesota. Inserts adapted from *Little Rock Catholic Study Bible*, © 2011 by Little Rock Scripture Study, Little Rock, Arkansas; additional inserts, prayers, and study questions by Little Rock Scripture Study staff, © 2023 by Order of Saint Benedict, Collegeville, Minnesota. All rights reserved. No part of this book may be used or reproduced in any manner whatsoever, except brief quotations in reviews, without written permission of Liturgical Press, Saint John's Abbey, PO Box 7500, Collegeville, MN 56321-7500. Printed in the United States of America.

1   2   3   4   5   6   7   8   9

Library of Congress Cataloging-in-Publication Data

Names: Hoppe, Leslie J., author. | Little Rock Scripture Study Staff, author.
Title: Isaiah / Leslie J. Hoppe with Little Rock Scripture Study staff.
Description: Collegeville, MN : Liturgical Press, [2023-] | Completed in 2 volumes. | Contents: v. 1. Isaiah 1-39 — v. 2. Isaiah 40-66. | Summary: "A Bible study on the book of Isaiah exploring the history, theology, and poetry of this prophetic work. Includes commentary, study and reflection questions, prayers, and access to online lectures"— Provided by publisher.
Identifiers: LCCN 2022028476 (print) | LCCN 2022028477 (ebook) | ISBN 9780814667118 (v. 1 ; trade paperback) | ISBN 9780814667149 (v. 2 ; trade paperback) | ISBN 9780814667132 (v. 1 ; epub) | ISBN 9780814667132 (v. 1 ; pdf) | ISBN 9780814667163 (v. 2 ; epub) | ISBN 9780814667163 (v. 2 ; pdf)
Subjects: LCSH: Bible. Isaiah—Textbooks.
Classification: LCC BS1515.55 .H67 2023 (print) | LCC BS1515.55 (ebook) | DDC 224/.106—dc23/eng/20220801
LC record available at https://lccn.loc.gov/2022028476
LC ebook record available at https://lccn.loc.gov/2022028477

TABLE OF CONTENTS

Welcome	7
What materials will you use?	8
How will you use these materials?	8
Map: The Persian Empire	11
Map: Jerusalem in the Time of the Old Testament	12
Lesson One (Introduction and Isaiah 40:1–43:8)	13
Lesson Two (Isaiah 43:9–46:13)	31
Lesson Three (Isaiah 47–50)	45
Lesson Four (Isaiah 51–55)	59
Lesson Five (Isaiah 56–61)	73
Lesson Six (Isaiah 62–66)	91
Praying with Your Group	106
Reflecting on Scripture	108

 Wrap-Up Lectures and Discussion Tips for Facilitators are available for each lesson at no charge. Find them online at LittleRockScripture.org/Lectures/IsaiahPartTwo.

Welcome

The Bible is at the heart of what it means to be a Christian. It is the Spirit-inspired word of God for us. It reveals to us the God who created, redeemed, and guides us still. It speaks to us personally and as a church. It forms the basis of our public liturgical life and our private prayer lives. It urges us to live worthily and justly, to love tenderly and wholeheartedly, and to be a part of building God's kingdom here on earth.

Though it was written a long time ago, in the context of a very different culture, the Bible is no relic of the past. Catholic biblical scholarship is among the best in the world, and in our time and place, we have unprecedented access to it. By making use of solid scholarship, we can discover much about the ancient culture and religious practices that shaped those who wrote the various books of the Bible. With these insights, and by praying with the words of Scripture, we allow the words and images to shape us as disciples. By sharing our journey of faithful listening to God's word with others, we have the opportunity to be stretched in our understanding and to form communities of love and learning. Ultimately, studying and praying with God's word deepens our relationship with Christ.

Isaiah, Part Two
Isaiah 40–66

The resource you hold in your hands is divided into six lessons. Each lesson involves personal prayer and study using this book and the experience of group prayer, discussion, and wrap-up lecture.

If you are using this resource in the context of a small group, we suggest that you meet six times, discussing one lesson per meeting. Allow about 90 minutes for the small group gathering. Small groups function best with eight to twelve people to ensure good group dynamics and to allow all to participate as they wish.

Some groups choose to have an initial gathering before their regular sessions begin. This allows an opportunity to meet one another, pass out books, and, if desired, view the optional intro lecture for this study available on the "Resources" page of the Little Rock Scripture Study website (www.littlerockscripture.org). Please note that there is only one intro lecture for two-part studies.

Every Bible study group is a little bit different. Some of our groups like to break each lesson up into two weeks of study so they are reading less each week and have more time to discuss the questions together at their weekly gatherings.

If your group wishes to do this, simply agree how much of each lesson will be read each week, and only answer the questions that correspond to the material you read. Wrap-up lectures can then be viewed at the end of every other meeting rather than at the end of every meeting. Of course, this will mean that your study will last longer, and your group will meet more times.

WHAT MATERIALS WILL YOU USE?

The materials in this book include:

- The text of Isaiah, chapters 40–66, using the New American Bible, Revised Edition as the translation.
- Commentary by Leslie J. Hoppe (which has also been published separately as part of the New Collegeville Bible Commentary series).
- Occasional inserts 🔥 highlighting elements of the chapters of Isaiah being studied. Some of these appear also in the *Little Rock Catholic Study Bible* while others are supplied by staff writers.
- Questions for study, reflection, and discussion at the end of each lesson.
- Opening and closing prayers for each lesson, as well as other prayer forms available in the closing pages of the book.

In addition, there are wrap-up lectures available for each lesson. Your group may choose to purchase a DVD containing these lectures or make use of the video lectures available online at no charge. The link to these free lectures is: LittleRockScripture.org/Lectures/IsaiahPartTwo. Of course, if your group has access to qualified speakers, you may choose to have live presentations.

Each person will need a current translation of the Bible. We recommend the *Little Rock Catholic Study Bible*, which makes use of the New American Bible, Revised Edition. Other translations, such as the New Jerusalem Bible or the New Revised Standard Version: Catholic Edition, would also work well.

HOW WILL YOU USE THESE MATERIALS?

Prepare in advance

Using Lesson One as an example:

- Begin with a simple prayer like the one found on page 13.

- Read the assigned material for Lesson One (pages 14–26) so that you are prepared for the weekly small group session.
- Answer the questions, Exploring Lesson One, found at the end of the assigned reading, pages 27–29.
- Use the Closing Prayer on page 30 when you complete your study. This prayer may be used again when you meet with the group.

Meet with your small group
- After introductions and greetings, allow time for prayer (about 5 minutes) as you begin the group session. You may use the prayer on page 13 (also used by individuals in their preparation) or use a prayer of your choosing.
- Spend about 45–50 minutes discussing the responses to the questions that were prepared in advance. You may also develop your discussion further by responding to questions and interests that arise during the discussion and faith-sharing itself.
- Close the discussion and faith-sharing with prayer, about 5–10 minutes. You may use the Closing Prayer at the end of each lesson or one of your choosing at the end of the book. It is important to allow people to pray for personal and community needs and to give thanks for how God is moving in your lives.
- Listen to or view the wrap-up lecture associated with each lesson (15–20 minutes). You may watch the lecture online, use a DVD, or provide a live lecture by a qualified local speaker. View the lecture together at the end of the session or, if your group runs out of time, you may invite group members to watch the lecture on their own time after the discussion.

A note to individuals
- If you are using this resource for individual study, simply move at your own pace. Take as much time as you need to read, study, and pray with the material.
- If you would like to share this experience with others, consider inviting a friend or family member to join you for your next study. Even a small group of two or three provides an opportunity for fruitful dialog and faith-sharing!

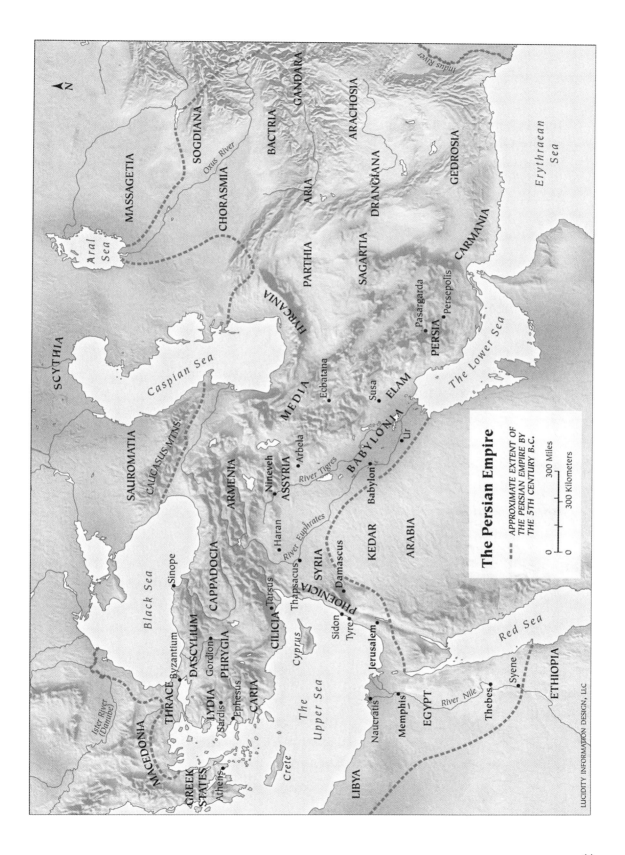

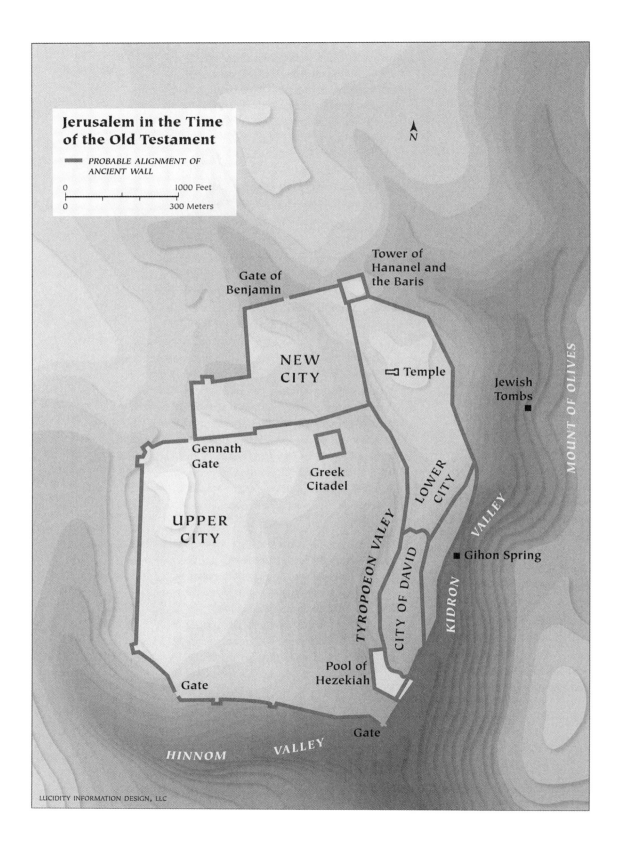

Isaiah

Part Two

LESSON ONE

Introduction and Isaiah 40:1–43:8

Begin your personal study and group discussion with a simple and sincere prayer such as:

Prayer

Lord God, as we continue our study of Isaiah, may our hearts remain open to the prophet's proclamation of your boundless love for your people. Inspire us with your Spirit so we may always be moved to seek you and to serve one another.

Read the Introduction on page 14 and the Bible text of Isaiah 40:1–43:8 found in the outside columns of pages 15–26, highlighting what stands out to you.

Read the accompanying commentary to add to your understanding.

Respond to the questions on pages 27–29, Exploring Lesson One.

The Closing Prayer on page 30 is for your personal use and may be used at the end of group discussion.

Lesson One

INTRODUCTION

Welcome to Part Two of Little Rock Scripture Study's *Isaiah*. Before beginning this in-depth exploration of Isaiah 40–66, a brief review of some themes that appeared in Part One of our study may be helpful. Many of the same themes will continue to be of importance as we explore the remainder of Isaiah's message.

In the early chapters of Isaiah, the prophet repeatedly upbraids Jerusalem for its infidelity (the worship of idols and, perhaps more importantly, a failure to observe the torah's commands for social justice). Through the prophet, God rejects mere ritualism as atonement for these faults: temple sacrifice alone will not satisfy God or placate divine anger, for what God seeks is not "the blood of calves, lambs, and goats" but true repentance and reformation (1:11-17). Although the entire city bears responsibility for the abandonment of the covenant, in the early oracles Isaiah most forcefully condemns the powerful and rich, who have disavowed their responsibility to the oppressed, focusing instead on their own advantage and pleasure. Through a series of effective metaphors, Isaiah predicts what the outcome of Jerusalem's continued obstinacy will be: the city will suffer the fate of an abandoned vineyard, its faithless rich will be devoured by the mouth of Sheol, and its inhabitants will fall victim to an enemy from a "far-off nation" (5:1-7, 14, 26-29).

Despite the savagery that seems to characterize God's vengeful judgments against Judah and the nations in passages such as Isaiah 13–24 and 30:27–31:9, Isaiah paints a complex and balanced portrait of God. Isaiah presents God as totally sovereign and completely separate from humankind ("the Holy One of Israel"). At the same time, however, God remains full of compassion and love for the people, even in their infidelity. As a result, interspersed among the dire predictions of ruin and exile awaiting Judah as punishment for its disobedience, the reader of Isaiah finds lyrical promises of salvation, renewal, and hope that will come only from the hands of God (35:1-10).

This multifaceted portrait of a God who is at the same time both punitive and loving persists in chapters 40–66, the focus of *Isaiah, Part Two*. In this portion of Isaiah, the reader may feel the prophet's emphasis subtly shifting toward the positive expectations of release from exile and return to God's favor. The instrument of this release will be the "servant" of the Lord, a shadowy figure that initially appears to be Cyrus the Great (called God's "anointed" in 45:1). Later mentions of this "servant," however, describe an agent of salvation very unlike any earthly king (see, for example, 52:13–53:12).

While idolatry continues to be denounced with devastating irony in chapters 40–55, more striking are Isaiah's descriptions of a renewed Jerusalem. Not that images of violence are completely lacking from the second part of Isaiah: the graphic and bloody description of God's punishment meted out to the enemies of Jerusalem matches or exceeds anything found in the earlier oracles (see, for example, 49:25-26; 63:3-6). The prophet presents such violence as a necessary prelude to the exaltation of Jerusalem/Zion, after which there will be universal peace in accordance with God's will (65:19-25).

As you begin your study of Isaiah 40–66, it is our hope that the essential messages of Isaiah—the necessity for repentance and the call to faithfulness toward God through an active concern for those most in need—will enrich your understanding of Scripture and will enhance your own life of prayer and action.

Lesson One

> **II. Isaiah 40–55**
>
> **CHAPTER 40**
>
> *Promise of Salvation*
>
> ¹Comfort, give comfort to my people,
>   says your God.
> ²Speak to the heart of Jerusalem, and
>   proclaim to her
>   that her service has ended,
>   that her guilt is expiated,
> That she has received from the hand of the
>   LORD
>   double for all her sins.
>
> *continue*

JERUSALEM'S LIBERATION

Isaiah 40:1–55:13

Here begins a thoroughly new message for Jerusalem. Unlike earlier prophets, the author of these words did not ask the people to recognize their failure and confess their infidelity. Before the exile, the prophets had to overcome the people's self-delusion fueled by the existence of the national state, the economic prosperity enjoyed by the powerful, and the active national cult in Jerusalem. The fall of that city made continued denials impossible. Judah's religious, political, and social institutions were no more. The Davidic dynasty was no more, the temple was in ruins and its priesthood scattered, the national state ceased to exist, and Judah's powerful and influential citizens were in exile. Cheap promises and vain expectations were no longer persuasive.

Chapter 40 begins a unique response to the disasters that came upon Jerusalem and its people. Unlike the book of Lamentations, the book of Isaiah does not give voice to the grief of the exiles. Unlike the Deuteronomistic History, this book is explicit about its hope for a new and glorious future for Jerusalem. Of course, the prophet believed that the fall of Jerusalem was an act of divine judgment on the unfaithful city, but he also was certain that the city's glorious and miraculous restoration was imminent. The prophet saw a dramatic upheaval stirring on the political horizon. A new vigorous and powerful ruler was about to bring an end to the vaunted Babylonian Empire. He believed that this was happening for one purpose: God was about to restore Jerusalem.

The prophet uses two metaphors to speak about his beliefs concerning Jerusalem's future: one masculine and the other feminine. The masculine servant metaphor (42:1-4; 49:1-6; 50:4-11; and 52:13–53:12) is the more familiar because of the use the New Testament makes of these passages to express faith in Jesus Christ. Like a king, the servant establishes justice (42:4). He is a "sharp-edged sword" and a "sharpened arrow" (49:2) whose suffering will benefit many (53:4-5) and who will be vindicated and then will divide out the spoils of war (53:12). The female figure of Jerusalem/Zion is the second linchpin of the prophet's hopes for the future. Beginning in chapter 49 and extending to chapter 66, the reader hears the story of a woman's life from her abandonment by her husband and consequent childlessness to their reconciliation and the birth of many children. The two images parallel one another. For example, in chapter 49 both express doubts

Lesson One

> ³A voice proclaims:
> In the wilderness prepare the way of the LORD!
>   Make straight in the wasteland a highway
>   for our God!
> ⁴Every valley shall be lifted up,
>   every mountain and hill made low;
> The rugged land shall be a plain,
>   the rough country, a broad valley.
> ⁵Then the glory of the LORD shall be revealed,
>   and all flesh shall see it together;
>   for the mouth of the LORD has spoken.
>
> ⁶A voice says, "Proclaim!"
>   I answer, "What shall I proclaim?"
> "All flesh is grass,
>   and all their loyalty like the flower of the
>   field.
> ⁷The grass withers, the flower wilts,
>   when the breath of the LORD blows upon
>   it."
> "Yes, the people is grass!
> ⁸The grass withers, the flower wilts,
>   but the word of our God stands forever."
>
> ⁹Go up onto a high mountain,
>   Zion, herald of good news!
> Cry out at the top of your voice,
>   Jerusalem, herald of good news!
> Cry out, do not fear!
>   Say to the cities of Judah:
>   Here is your God!
> ¹⁰Here comes with power
>   the Lord GOD,
>   who rules by his strong arm;
>
> *continue*

40:1-11 Jerusalem the herald

The prophet stands as a mute witness as the members of the Divine Council are about to implement God's decision to begin the process of Jerusalem's rehabilitation. The prophet hears a series of commands in the second person plural: "comfort . . . Speak to the heart of . . . proclaim. . . ." He wishes his readers to envision one member of the Divine Council ordering others to take the actions that will mean a new day for Jerusalem. This new day will begin with the news that the city's suffering is about to end. In fact, the order implies that Jerusalem's punishment has been more than its infidelity deserved. Next, the prophet hears one member of the council commanding that another begin preparing the way for God's grand triumphal procession that will bring about the exiles' return and Jerusalem's restoration. The death-dealing nature of the desert must teem with life. The high mountains and deep valleys that would hinder the return of the exiles to Jerusalem must become a level highway.

Jerusalem was not to remain a passive recipient of the good news. The city itself was to become a prophet announcing liberation to the other cities of Judah, which shared its fate during the Babylonian crisis. They too lost many people to exile. Zion is to proclaim the great reversal that God is about to accomplish. God is returning to Judah at the head of a great throng of exiles, who were coming home where they could live in freedom as God promised their ancestors. In fulfilling its prophetic mission, Jerusalem uses two metaphors to remove the doubts of those who believed that God had no concern for Judah. In verse 10, the city-turned-prophet presents God as a victorious general who is returning home with the exiles—the prize won by defeating the Babylonians. The image in verse 11 is the perfect counterpoint, for it depicts God as a gentle shepherd who takes care of newborn lambs, leading them back to their mothers. Just so God will lead back the exiles of Judah to their mothers—the cities of their homeland. The juxtaposition of these two metaphors affirms that God has the power to change the course of history

about God's presence and power in their lives: the servant in verse 4 and Zion in verse 14. Both the servant and Zion are humiliated and afflicted. Eventually both will experience vindication through their children: the servant in 53:10 and Zion in 66:7-9. The prophet does not tell the story of the servant or of Zion as a continuous narrative but will keep returning to these metaphors in the course of his prophecy.

but is still concerned about the exiles as individuals. The exiles needed to hear what both metaphors implied, since their primary experience of God had been the experience of God's absence. This led them to draw all the wrong conclusions about their future. Jerusalem proclaims that God has the power to end the exile and the love to begin the restoration.

The image of **God as a shepherd** who gathers and cares for the flock of Israel (40:11) is common in the Old Testament and can be found in Wisdom literature (Sir 18:13), the prophets (Jer 31:10) and Psalms (23, 80, 95, 100). These biblical texts highlight various aspects of the shepherd's role. For example, Genesis 49:24 and Jeremiah 31:10 emphasize protection, while God's sustaining care is the focus of Psalm 95:7. In Ezekiel 34:11-16, the messianic role of gathering and healing is emphasized. The description of Jesus as the good shepherd in John's Gospel (10:11-16) encompasses all these Old Testament meanings.

Chapter 40:1-11 sums up the prophet's message in just eleven verses. This text makes the astonishing announcement that God has forgiven Jerusalem and its people. It is Jerusalem's task to proclaim this message to all the cities of Judah. The remainder of chapters 40–55 is simply an elaboration of that message.

Each of the evangelists cites 40:3, applying it to John the Baptist (Matt 3:3; Mark 1:2; Luke 3:4; John 1:23). Of course, this involves a reinterpretation of the prophet's words. No longer do they refer simply to the restoration of Jerusalem but to the redemption of all Israel and all nations. The evangelists wish to portray the Baptist as the herald of this new and universal act of salvation. James alludes to verses 6-7 to speak of the transitory nature of wealth (Jas 1:10) and Peter quotes these verses to underscore the eternal character of God's word (1 Pet 1:24-25).

> Here is his reward with him,
>   his recompense before him.
> ¹¹Like a shepherd he feeds his flock;
>   in his arms he gathers the lambs,
> Carrying them in his bosom,
>   leading the ewes with care.
>
> *Power of God and the Vanity of Idols*
>
> ¹²Who has measured with his palm the waters,
>   marked off the heavens with a span,
>   held in his fingers the dust of the earth,
>   weighed the mountains in scales
>   and the hills in a balance?
> ¹³Who has directed the spirit of the LORD,
>   or instructed him as his counselor?
> ¹⁴Whom did he consult to gain knowledge?
>   Who taught him the path of judgment,
>   or showed him the way of understanding?
>
> ¹⁵See, the nations count as a drop in the bucket,
>   as a wisp of cloud on the scales;
>   the coastlands weigh no more than a speck.
> ¹⁶Lebanon would not suffice for fuel,
>   nor its animals be enough for burnt offerings.
>
> *continue*

40:12-31 The Lord, the Creator

To arouse the exiles to believe in a future for Jerusalem, the prophet begins with correcting and expanding their notion of deity. The Lord was not simply a God from the desert who chose to make a nation out of the Hebrew slaves. The Lord is not simply the patron of the two former Israelite kingdoms. By asking a series of rhetorical questions in verses 12-14, the prophet leads the exiles to the conclusion that the Lord is the Creator of the universe. As such, Jerusalem's God controls the destinies of all nations. Of course, the Lord has the power to end the exile and return the people of Jerusalem to their home.

¹⁷Before him all the nations are as nought,
  as nothing and void he counts them.

¹⁸To whom can you liken God?
  With what likeness can you confront him?
¹⁹An idol? An artisan casts it,
  the smith plates it with gold,
  fits it with silver chains.
²⁰Is mulberry wood the offering?
  A skilled artisan picks out
  a wood that will not rot,
  Seeks to set up for himself
  an idol that will not totter.

²¹Do you not know? Have you not heard?
  Was it not told you from the beginning?
  Have you not understood from the
    founding of the earth?
²²The one who is enthroned above the vault
    of the earth,
  its inhabitants like grasshoppers,
Who stretches out the heavens like a veil
  and spreads them out like a tent to dwell in,
²³Who brings princes to nought
  and makes the rulers of the earth as
    nothing.
²⁴Scarcely are they planted, scarcely sown,
  scarcely their stem rooted in the earth,
When he breathes upon them and they
    wither,
  and the stormwind carries them away like
    straw.

continue

By way of contrast, the gods of the nations are nothing. A second series of rhetorical questions in verses 18-20 parodies the religious beliefs of the nations. The prophet compares the God of Israel, the Creator of the universe, with the gods of the nations who were manufactured by wood and metal workers. Of course, the people of the ancient Near East had a more nuanced view of the relationship between a god and its image than the prophet implies. Still, the prophet's purpose is not to discuss the merits of religions that use images. His purpose is to stimulate his people to believe in their future, a future made possible by the Creator of the universe, who controls the fate of all nations.

The prophet undercuts belief in astral deities by having Israel's God claim credit for the creation of the stars. It is the Lord who maintains the order of the heavens, and every heavenly body is subject to the God who is about to redeem Jerusalem. The profound and distressing experience of God's absence that led the exiles to question the power of the Lord and the relevance of their faith will dissipate in the face of the stirring events that will shortly and dramatically demonstrate the presence and power of the Lord: the fall of Babylon and the restoration of Jerusalem. These events will quicken the spirits of the exiles and prevent Judah from disappearing into the pages of history. The people of God will find new strength as they await their return to the land that God promised to their ancestors.

Paul quotes verse 13 in his hymn to God's mercy and wisdom in Romans 11:34-35. He also

The **structure of Isaiah 40:12-31** is defined by questions. The prophet is emphasizing a major point: God has both the power and the will to deliver the people from the Babylonian exile.

Who is this?	The all-powerful Creator of the whole world (vv. 12-17).
"To whom can you liken God?"	Idols are just wood or metal (vv. 18-20).
"Do you not know? Have you not heard?"	The Creator is greater than all earthly power (vv. 21-24).
"To whom can you liken me . . . ?"	The Creator of sun and stars (considered by Babylon to be gods) can certainly help Israel (vv. 25-27).
"Do you not know? Have you not heard?"	The Creator will strengthen you (vv. 28-31).

cites this text again in 1 Corinthians 2:16 to celebrate the revelation of God's will through Jesus Christ.

41:1–42:9 The nations on trial

A typical prophetic strategy to underscore the sovereignty of God is to describe a trial in which God serves as prosecutor and judge. Here the prophet describes two such scenes in which the nations are on trial. The prophet wants to present the restoration of Judah to its land against a wider backdrop. He calls the nations to hear his message for they too will feel the effects of God's new movement, whose ultimate goal is the redemption of God's people.

The evidence of God's control of events that will lead to Jerusalem's liberation is the rise of the person whom the prophet characterizes as "the champion of justice." He comes not from Judah but from the East (41:2). Cyrus the Persian was on the march, winning victories over the Medes and the Greeks. The prophet was certain that Babylon was about to fall to him as well. This string of victories must mean something. The prophet sees them as a sign of God's movement to save Judah and restore it to its land. It is Judah's God who is transforming the political map of the ancient Near East—all for the sake of Jerusalem. This is certainly evidence of the power of the Lord.

The imminent fall of Babylon is not the end of the first trial scene. The scene ends with a dramatic reassurance for the exiles. The prophet speaks to the exiles in God's name. They have nothing to fear from the military and political upheavals that they are witnessing. On the contrary, all is happening for their sake. God has chosen Israel and has not revoked that choice. The prophet calls the exiles the "offspring of Abraham" because he wishes to underscore the continuing significance of Israel's ancestral religious traditions (41:8). With God's help, Judah will be victorious over all those forces that threaten its existence.

²⁵To whom can you liken me as an equal?
  says the Holy One.
²⁶Lift up your eyes on high
  and see who created these:
He leads out their army and numbers them,
  calling them all by name.
By his great might and the strength of his power
  not one of them is missing!
²⁷Why, O Jacob, do you say,
  and declare, O Israel,
"My way is hidden from the LORD,
  and my right is disregarded by my God"?
²⁸Do you not know?
  Have you not heard?
The LORD is God from of old,
  creator of the ends of the earth.
He does not faint or grow weary,
  and his knowledge is beyond scrutiny.
²⁹He gives power to the faint,
  abundant strength to the weak.
³⁰Though young men faint and grow weary,
  and youths stagger and fall,
³¹They that hope in the LORD will renew their strength,
  they will soar on eagles' wings;
They will run and not grow weary,
  walk and not grow faint.

CHAPTER 41

The Liberator of Israel

¹Keep silence before me, O coastlands;
  let the nations renew their strength.
Let them draw near and speak;
  let us come together for judgment.
²Who has stirred up from the East the champion of justice,
  and summoned him to be his attendant?
To him he delivers nations
  and subdues kings;
With his sword he reduces them to dust,
  with his bow, to driven straw.
³He pursues them, passing on without loss,
  by a path his feet scarcely touch.

continue

⁴Who has performed these deeds?
   Who has called forth the generations
      from the beginning?
I, the LORD, am the first,
   and at the last I am he.
⁵The coastlands see, and fear;
   the ends of the earth tremble:
   they approach, they come on.

⁶Each one helps his neighbor,
   one says to the other, "Courage!"
⁷The woodworker encourages the goldsmith,
   the one who beats with the hammer, him
      who strikes on the anvil,
Saying of the soldering, "It is good!"
   then fastening it with nails so it will not
      totter.

⁸But you, Israel, my servant,
   Jacob, whom I have chosen,
   offspring of Abraham my friend—
⁹You whom I have taken from the ends of the
      earth
   and summoned from its far-off places,
To whom I have said, You are my servant;
   I chose you, I have not rejected you—
¹⁰Do not fear: I am with you;
   do not be anxious: I am your God.
I will strengthen you, I will help you,
   I will uphold you with my victorious right
      hand.

¹¹Yes, all shall be put to shame and disgrace
   who vent their anger against you;
Those shall be as nothing and perish
   who offer resistance.
¹²You shall seek but not find
   those who strive against you;
They shall be as nothing at all
   who do battle with you.

¹³For I am the LORD, your God,
   who grasp your right hand;
It is I who say to you, Do not fear,
   I will help you.
¹⁴Do not fear, you worm Jacob,

continue

While Isaiah's emphasis on God's plan for the salvation of the **"offspring of Abraham"** (41:8-10) specifically refers to the people of Israel, this in no way contradicts the universalism of God's plan for salvation found elsewhere in Isaiah (see 49:6; 56:1-8; 60:3; 66:18). As Paul will explain in Galatians centuries later, all who have faith in God's word, whether Jew or Gentile, can account themselves "children of Abraham" (3:7).

Judah's political impotence will have no bearing on its future. God will be with Judah to insure that it will emerge victorious. It is important to note that the book's favorite term for God, "the Holy One of Israel," is used here with the word "redeemer" (41:14). This will happen several other times in this fourth section of Isaiah (see also 43:14; 47:3-4; 48:17). The book of Isaiah refers to God as "redeemer" more than any other book of the Old Testament. Israel's redeemer will transform it into a power that will overcome those that will try to prevent its restoration. It will emerge with unprecedented power over its enemies. Judah will be able to crush them like a new threshing sledge cuts through the newly harvested shafts of wheat.

While Isaiah's use of the terms **"worm" and "maggot"** in reference to Israel (41:14) may seem jarring, the words serve a dual purpose. Both terms suggest death and decay, which the prophet believes would be inevitable for Israel without God's aid. Both expressions also remind the reader of the tremendous gulf separating humanity from the Holy One of Israel. Isaiah is stressing that deliverance from enemies will not come to Israel through any effort of its own but only by the might of God's "victorious right hand" (41:10-12).

God's movement on behalf of the oppressed of Judah will be a miraculous manifestation of God's power. It will be akin to the transformation of the desert into a well-watered garden graced with every beautiful tree and shrub. No one who will witness Judah's restoration will fail to understand who accomplished this miracle—the Holy One of Israel. The results of the trial of the nations will be the restoration of Jerusalem and the universal recognition of its God.

There is a summons to a second trial in 41:21. The prophet begins offering evidence in the next verse. That evidence consists of the rise of Cyrus, the fall of Babylon, and the restoration of Jerusalem. People had recourse to their gods to divine the future. The prophet ridicules the supposed ability of the gods to inform their worshipers about the future. Who would have predicted that Judah would be restored to its land? But that is precisely what is about to take place. The events that are to occur in a short time will shame the so-called gods of the nations. None of their diviners could have foreseen what God has in store for Jerusalem. Events are unfolding. Cyrus is coming to bring an end to Judah's exile. Jerusalem will no longer be a forlorn, abandoned city. It is to be the herald announcing freedom to the exiles. Clearly, the gods of the nations are nothing.

 A **threshing sledge** (41:15) is a wooden frame or board whose underside is studded with sharp points made of metal or some other jagged material. The board is hauled over crops to separate the grain from the stalks. In Job, the belly of Leviathan (a mythical beast identified by some scholars with the crocodile) is likened to a threshing sledge covered with fragments of sharp pottery (Job 41:22).

A threshing sledge

you maggot Israel;
I will help you—oracle of the LORD;
    the Holy One of Israel is your redeemer.
¹⁵I will make of you a threshing sledge,
    sharp, new, full of teeth,
To thresh the mountains and crush them,
    to make the hills like chaff.
¹⁶When you winnow them, the wind shall carry them off,
    the storm shall scatter them.
But you shall rejoice in the LORD;
    in the Holy One of Israel you shall glory.

¹⁷The afflicted and the needy seek water in vain,
    their tongues are parched with thirst.
I, the LORD, will answer them;
    I, the God of Israel, will not forsake them.
¹⁸I will open up rivers on the bare heights,
    and fountains in the broad valleys;
I will turn the wilderness into a marshland,
    and the dry ground into springs of water.
¹⁹In the wilderness I will plant the cedar,
    acacia, myrtle, and olive;
In the wasteland I will set the cypress,
    together with the plane tree and the pine,
²⁰That all may see and know,
    observe and understand,
That the hand of the LORD has done this,
    the Holy One of Israel has created it.

²¹Present your case, says the LORD;
    bring forward your arguments, says the King of Jacob.
²²Let them draw near and foretell to us
    what it is that shall happen!
What are the things of long ago?
    Tell us, that we may reflect on them
    and know their outcome;
Or declare to us the things to come,
    ²³tell what is to be in the future,
    that we may know that you are gods!
Do something, good or evil,
    that will put us in awe and in fear.

continue

> ²⁴Why, you are nothing
>   and your work is nought;
>   to choose you is an abomination!
>
> ²⁵I have stirred up one from the north, and
>   he comes;
>   from the east I summon him by name;
> He shall trample the rulers down like mud,
>   like a potter treading clay.
> ²⁶Who announced this from the beginning,
>   that we might know;
>   beforehand, that we might say, "True"?
> Not one of you foretold it, not one spoke;
>   not one heard you say,
> ²⁷"The first news for Zion: here they come,"
>   or, "I will give Jerusalem a herald of good
>   news."
> ²⁸When I look, there is not one,
>   not one of them to give counsel,
>   to make an answer when I question them.
> ²⁹Ah, all of them are nothing,
>   their works are nought,
>   their idols, empty wind!
>
> **CHAPTER 42**
>
> *The Servant of the Lord*
>
> ¹Here is my servant whom I uphold,
>   my chosen one with whom I am pleased.
> Upon him I have put my spirit;
>   he shall bring forth justice to the nations.
> ²He will not cry out, nor shout,
>   nor make his voice heard in the street.
> ³A bruised reed he will not break,
>   and a dimly burning wick he will not
>   quench.
>   He will faithfully bring forth justice.
> ⁴He will not grow dim or be bruised
>   until he establishes justice on the earth;
>   the coastlands will wait for his teaching.
> ⁵Thus says God, the LORD,
>   who created the heavens and stretched
>   them out,
>
> *continue*

The **miraculous gift of water** promised by God in 41:17-18 symbolizes God's power to vivify, restore, and transform. The prophet Jeremiah speaks of God as a source of "living waters" (Jer 2:13; 17:13) and Jesus identifies himself with the Father as a source of "living water . . . welling up to eternal life" (John 4:10-14; see also 7:37-38).

The trial ends with a reaffirmation of the election of Israel as God's people. God's choice of Israel is a fundamental datum of its faith. But this belief was called into question by the fall of the two Israelite kingdoms. The prophet's message implies that Israel's election is not tied to the political status of the two former kingdoms. Judah in exile is still God's servant. It has a destiny to fulfill that cannot be frustrated by political turmoil and military defeat. God will restore Judah to its land so that it can become a model of justice for the nations. The Israelite kingdoms fell precisely because of the failure of the monarchy to maintain a just social and economic system. Judah's mission to establish justice is repeated three times (42:1, 4, 6).

Note that the prophet does not imply that the monarchy will be restored. The establishment and maintenance of a just society were the principal responsibilities of Israel's kings. The book of Isaiah very clearly notes the failure of the monarchy to do this. In fact, Israel's political leadership actually facilitated the oppression of the poor (e.g., 1:21-23; 3:1-12; 28:14-22; 29:14-15). Here the responsibilities of the monarchy fall upon the people as a whole. It will be the responsibility of all the people of Judah to insure "the victory of justice." The trial of the nations ends with an affirmation of God's uniqueness. Only the Lord has announced the liberation of Jerusalem's exiles—something everyone, including those exiles, thought impossible. This shows that the Lord alone is God.

Chapter 42:1-4 is the first of four passages from the book of Isaiah that have become known as the "Servant Songs" (see also 49:1-6; 50:4-11; and 52:13–53:12). While there is some value in isolating these passages, here they will be treated simply as elements in the broader and unified message about Jerusalem's liberation that comprises the fourth section of the book of Isaiah. There has been some controversy about the propriety of isolating these texts from their literary and theological context, and there are several possibilities about the identity of the "servant." Understood in the light of the total argument made in this fourth section, it is most likely that the servant is Judah fulfilling its destiny to be the light to the nations, bringing about the victory of justice. Of course, this is an idealized picture of the potential of the restored community, but the whole of this fourth section of Isaiah is a powerfully constructed and expressed argument by the prophet, who is trying to persuade a thoroughly demoralized people that their God is about to do something wondrous for them and that they have a decisive role in their own restoration.

John the Baptist warns that God's "winnowing fan is in his hand" (Matt 3:12; cf. Isa 41:16).

who spread out the earth and its produce,
Who gives breath to its people
    and spirit to those who walk on it:
⁶I, the Lord, have called you for justice,
    I have grasped you by the hand;
I formed you, and set you
    as a covenant for the people,
    a light for the nations,
⁷To open the eyes of the blind,
    to bring out prisoners from confinement,
    and from the dungeon, those who live in darkness.
⁸I am the Lord, Lord is my name;
    my glory I give to no other,
    nor my praise to idols.
⁹See, the earlier things have come to pass,
    new ones I now declare;
Before they spring forth
    I announce them to you.

The Lord's Purpose for Israel

¹⁰Sing to the Lord a new song,
    his praise from the ends of the earth:
Let the sea and what fills it resound,
    the coastlands, and those who dwell in them.
¹¹Let the wilderness and its cities cry out,
    the villages where Kedar dwells;
Let the inhabitants of Sela exult,
    and shout from the top of the mountains.
¹²Let them give glory to the Lord,
    and utter his praise in the coastlands.

¹³The Lord goes forth like a warrior,
    like a man of war he stirs up his fury;
He shouts out his battle cry,
    against his enemies he shows his might:
¹⁴For a long time I have kept silent,
    I have said nothing, holding myself back;
Now I cry out like a woman in labor,
    gasping and panting.
¹⁵I will lay waste mountains and hills,
    all their undergrowth I will dry up;

continue

> I will turn the rivers into marshes,
>   and the marshes I will dry up.
> ¹⁶I will lead the blind on a way they do not know;
>   by paths they do not know I will guide them.
> I will turn darkness into light before them,
>   and make crooked ways straight.
> These are my promises:
>   I made them, I will not forsake them.
>
> ¹⁷They shall be turned back in utter shame
>   who trust in idols;
> Who say to molten images,
>   "You are our gods."
> ¹⁸You deaf ones, listen,
>   you blind ones, look and see!
> ¹⁹Who is blind but my servant,
>   or deaf like the messenger I send?
> Who is blind like the one I restore,
>   blind like the servant of the LORD?
> ²⁰You see many things but do not observe;
>   ears open, but do not hear.
> ²¹It was the LORD's will for the sake of his justice
>   to make his teaching great and glorious.
>
> ²²This is a people plundered and despoiled,
>   all of them trapped in holes,
>   hidden away in prisons.
> They are taken as plunder, with no one to rescue them,
>   as spoil, with no one to say, "Give back!"
> ²³Who among you will give ear to this,
>   listen and pay attention from now on?
> ²⁴Who was it that gave Jacob to be despoiled,
>   Israel to the plunderers?
> Was it not the LORD, against whom we have sinned?
> In his ways they refused to walk,
>   his teaching they would not heed.
> ²⁵So he poured out wrath upon them,
>
> *continue*

Matthew has John the Baptist allude to 41:16 to persuade people that God is about to do something decisive through Jesus (Matt 3:12). The evangelist also cites 42:1-4 to show that Jesus' healing ministry fulfilled the words of the prophet and, therefore, show Jesus to be the "servant" about whom the prophet was speaking (Matt 12:15-21). Simeon's canticle in Luke 2:29-32 is a combination of texts taken from the fourth section of the book of Isaiah: 42:6; 46:13; 49:6; 52:10.

42:10-17 The Lord, the Victor

The prophet sings a hymn of praise to the Lord who is about to liberate the exiles of Jerusalem. This, in turn, will lead all nations to acclaim the Lord as God. The hymn is reminiscent of several similar compositions found in the Psalter (Pss 93, 96, 149). The hymn begins with a call to praise that includes all regions of earth and sea—even remote and isolated places like Kedar and Sela. The call goes out to join in praising the Lord because Israel's God has finally chosen to emerge from self-imposed inactivity. God will now deal with God's enemies. Those who serve other gods will recognize their folly.

Two features of this hymn call for comment because both cause problems for some modern readers of Isaiah. The first is the hymn's military imagery. The people who first heard or read this book felt much more at ease with this imagery than do people today. After all, the origins of Israel were associated with battles that God fought and won: the victory over the Egyptian army at the Red Sea, the victories over the Canaanites during the time of Joshua and the judges, and the victories over the Philistines during the time of David. Judah was in exile because apparently God stopped taking its side against its enemies. This metaphor affirms that God's purposes are fulfilled—even in the wars that people fight over land and resources. It is important to remember that the Lord, the warrior, was not the only way that ancient Israel spoke of its God. The Lord was also the shepherd, who gathers the lambs, carries them gently, and feeds them abundantly (see Isa 40:11). While the New Testament speaks about Jesus as the "good shepherd" (John 10), it also remembers that Jesus said that he came to bring fire on the earth and could not wait until the blaze begins (see Luke 12:49).

A second metaphor in this passage compares the Lord to "a woman in labor" (42:14). Though most of the images that the Bible uses for God are masculine, the book of Isaiah does make use of feminine imagery to speak of the God of Israel (see also 49:15). The prophet did not hesitate to use feminine metaphors to speak of the God of Israel despite the patriarchal bent of his culture.

42:18—43:8 Judah's disabilities

The prophet recognizes to whom he is speaking. His audience is made up of people in shock, people still coping with the loss of the political, social, economic, and religious institutions that gave them identity and purpose. What is worse is that these people fail to recognize that they are responsible for this loss. The prophet calls the people of Judah blind and deaf. These handicaps prevent them from recognizing their true standing before God. They are unable to recognize God's hand in their plight. They fail to see that the loss of their state, national dynasty, temple, and land was due to their refusal to "walk in God's ways," i.e., maintain a society built on justice. They fail to hear the message of the prophets who announced God's judgment on their society and its values.

Still, the prophet believes that Judah's future is not dependent upon its ability to overcome its blindness and deafness. God will save Judah from its own sin. The prophet affirms that God will allow Cyrus to take Egypt and Ethiopia as the price for Judah's freedom. Here the prophet's word reflects the scandal of election: God favors one people over all others. The only explanation that the prophet gives is that God loves the people of Israel and will do anything to save Israel from itself. God assures

> his anger, and the fury of battle;
> It blazed all around them, yet they did not realize,
> it burned them, but they did not take it to heart.
>
> ## CHAPTER 43
>
> ### Promises of Redemption and Restoration
>
> ¹But now, thus says the LORD,
> who created you, Jacob, and formed you, Israel:
> Do not fear, for I have redeemed you;
> I have called you by name: you are mine.
> ²When you pass through waters, I will be with you;
> through rivers, you shall not be swept away.
> When you walk through fire, you shall not be burned,
> nor will flames consume you.
> ³For I, the LORD, am your God,
> the Holy One of Israel, your savior.
> I give Egypt as ransom for you,
> Ethiopia and Seba in exchange for you.
> ⁴Because you are precious in my eyes
> and honored, and I love you,
> I give people in return for you
> and nations in exchange for your life.
> ⁵Fear not, for I am with you;
> from the east I will bring back your offspring,
> from the west I will gather you.
> ⁶I will say to the north: Give them up!
> and to the south: Do not hold them!
> Bring back my sons from afar,
> and my daughters from the ends of the earth:
> ⁷All who are called by my name
> I created for my glory;
> I formed them, made them.
> ⁸Lead out the people, blind though they have eyes,
> deaf though they have ears.

Lesson One

Judah that the exiles will gather from wherever they have been scattered, even though they still suffer from handicaps. The prophet affirms that God is willing to allow the conquest of nations like Egypt and Ethiopia in exchange for Jerusalem's liberation. How does this relate to the prophet's contention that God's chosen servant is to be a "light to the nations"? The significance of the prophet's concept of Israel's election is one of the principal problems in interpreting this book. Even the New Testament's more consistent inclusiveness does not solve the problem. There God does not give up Egypt, Ethiopia, or any nation for Israel's salvation. But God does not spare Jesus so that all people might be saved. Why was it necessary for Jesus to die in order for the New Israel to be saved from the power of sin? Here we see this important issue in Christian theology presaged in the book of Isaiah.

The commentary's use of **"scandal"** in the phrase "scandal of election" may be unfamiliar. In common usage today, "scandal" almost always refers to a reprehensible act that causes public outrage. As a theological term, however, "scandal" (from the Greek, *skandalon*, a "snare" or "stumbling block") refers to ideas or conduct that may confuse or weaken the faith of another (see, for example, 1 Cor 1:23).

Readers today may find Isaiah's insistence on God's preference of Israel above all other nations troubling (43:1-7), but this divine preference must be considered in light of other passages that proclaim God's resolve to extend salvation to all nations (see 42:6; 51:4; 60:3).

Lesson One

EXPLORING LESSON ONE

1. How do the words of 40:2 provide the comfort that is spoken of in 40:1? (See 49:13.)

2. a) What image from Israel's history is evoked by referencing the way of the Lord in the wilderness (40:3-4)? (See Exod 13:21-22; Deut 2:7.)

   b) Isaiah 40:3-4 is adapted slightly and used in the Gospels in reference to the ministry of John the Baptist. What variations do you notice in the Gospel versions? How do Isaiah's words apply to John the Baptist? (See Matt 3:3; Mark 1:2-3; Luke 3:2-6; John 1:23.)

3. When have you experienced the lasting power of God's word in Scripture (40:6)? Can you offer an example of how God's word from an ancient time has been effective or meaningful in your life today?

Lesson One

4. Jerusalem is not simply rescued for its own sake but is given a commission for the sake of all Judah. What does this tell you about the nature of God's work in our individual and communal lives?

5. How does the prophet demonstrate that God is both powerful and gentle regarding the people in exile (40:10-11)?

6. a) Who is the "champion of justice" referenced in 41:2, and what can you learn about him? (See 44:28–45:1; 2 Chr 36:23-24; Ezra 1:2-4.)

   b) Has there ever been a time when you felt God used someone unexpected, or someone outside of our faith tradition, to teach a valuable lesson or to do God's work?

7. a) At the time Isaiah wrote 42:1-4, to whom might these words have been referring?

Lesson One

b) Why are these verses (42:1-4) and other "Servant Songs" (49:1-6; 50:4-11; 52:13–53:12) applied to Jesus in New Testament times?

8. Isaiah 42:6-7 offers a powerful summary of the role of God's covenant people. We, too, are God's covenant people (see Eph 2:13-20; 3:4-6). In what ways do these verses reflect or challenge the role of the church in our day and age?

9. Which of the metaphors or images of God found in the hymn of 42:10-17 is most appealing to you and why?

10. Isaiah 43:1-9 shifts to a message of hope and redemption, reminding Jacob/Israel that they belong to God. Which verse or phrase from this section resonates with you most deeply? Consider committing it to memory as a reminder of your own value to God.

CLOSING PRAYER

Prayer

*Do not fear: I am with you;
do not be anxious: I am your God.
I will strengthen you, I will help you,
I will uphold you with my victorious right
hand.* (Isa 41:10)

God our Father, there is so much in life that fills us with anxiety. We dread the threat of war, the prospect of illness, the specter of suffering, and the inevitability of death. Amid all these apprehensions, teach us to rely on you and your promises. May we come to realize that the only thing we should truly fear is separating ourselves from you. Help us to live lives of courage and hope, especially by . . .

LESSON TWO

Isaiah 43:9–46:13

Begin your personal study and group discussion with a simple and sincere prayer such as:

Prayer

Lord God, as we continue our study of Isaiah, may our hearts remain open to the prophet's proclamation of your boundless love for your people. Inspire us with your Spirit so we may always be moved to seek you and to serve one another.

Read the Bible text of Isaiah 43:9–46:13 found in the outside columns of pages 32–40, highlighting what stands out to you.

Read the accompanying commentary to add to your understanding.

Respond to the questions on pages 41–43, Exploring Lesson Two.

The Closing Prayer on page 44 is for your personal use and may be used at the end of group discussion.

Lesson Two

⁹Let all the nations gather together,
   let the peoples assemble!
Who among them could have declared this,
   or announced to us the earlier things?
Let them produce witnesses to prove
    themselves right,
   that one may hear and say, "It is true!"
¹⁰You are my witnesses—oracle of the LORD—
   my servant whom I have chosen
To know and believe in me
   and understand that I am he.
Before me no god was formed,
   and after me there shall be none.
¹¹I, I am the LORD;
   there is no savior but me.
¹²It is I who declared, who saved,
   who announced, not some strange god
    among you;
You are my witnesses—oracle of the LORD.
   I am God,
¹³yes, from eternity I am he;
There is none who can deliver from my hand:
   I act and who can cancel it?

¹⁴Thus says the LORD, your redeemer,
   the Holy One of Israel:
For your sake I send to Babylon;
   I will bring down all her defenses,
   and the Chaldeans shall cry out in
    lamentation.
¹⁵I am the LORD, your Holy One,
   the creator of Israel, your King.
¹⁶Thus says the LORD,
   who opens a way in the sea,
   a path in the mighty waters,

continue

43:9-15 Judah—God's witness

The prophet returns to the metaphor of a trial. The issue at hand is the Lord's claim to be God. How could people take this claim seriously when Judah was in exile? Of what value is a God who cannot protect or save? The liberation of Jerusalem will change people's views, so it is important that the exiles enthusiastically respond to the prophet's message of their imminent redemption. Of course, no one could have foreseen the circumstances that led to Judah's freedom. The prophet has consistently asserted that judgment was not God's last word to Jerusalem. He described a restored Zion and now his words are about to be fulfilled. The exiles are to put flesh and bone on those words and thereby become God's witnesses.

Judah's witnessing does not consist of providing rational proofs for God's existence. What Judah will show is God's power to save. When Judah had a king, the king's successes manifested God's power. But now the miraculous return of the exiles to Jerusalem will show the nations that Israel's God is God alone. The restoration of Jerusalem will be an irrefutable proof of the Lord's power to save. The fact of the exile appears to have undercut the credibility of Israel's witness. How could Israel's God claim any status given the fall of Jerusalem and the exile of its people? But the exile itself is a testament to God's sovereignty, since it was God who sent Israel to Babylon, but now that tragic episode in Israel's life is about to end. The Babylonians, on the other hand, will lament the fall of their city.

43:16–44:5 Something new

God's victory over the powers of nature during the exodus from Egypt has already shown God's might (Exod 7:8–11:10; 14:21), but these wondrous deeds are not simply memories. God will again act for Israel's sake. For the prophet, the exodus became a prototype of the restoration. Though the two events were separated from each other by hundreds of years, he was certain that the former illuminated the latter. God will free the exiles, lead them through the wilderness again, and bring them back to Jerusalem, where their praise of God's glory will be an effective witness to the one God. This new act of deliverance will be so spectacular that people will no longer remember the exodus but will recall with wonder and praise this new act of God's saving power. Just as the prophet reinterpreted the exodus story in terms of the exiles' experience, so did the New Testament reinterpret that same story as a way to speak of the significance of Jesus. The hymns of the African-American Christian community followed the same pattern, as does the liberation theology of the Americas. The prophet has shown many generations of believers how the exodus can always be something new.

Scholars have long debated the identity of the **"first father"** mentioned in 43:27. In 51:2, Abraham is designated as the father of Israel, but there is no record in Scripture of Abraham having grievously sinned against the Lord (in fact, 41:8 refers to Abraham as the "friend" of God). Jacob is a more likely candidate, given that he fathered the twelve tribes of Israel and was also accused of crimes against his brother Esau and rebellion against God (see Deut 32:15-18; Jer 9:3; Hos 12:2-7).

Unfortunately, God's liberation of the Hebrew slaves from Egypt did not produce a grateful people. They constantly murmured in the wilderness on the way to the promised land, and they rebelled against Moses. This pattern continued once Israel arrived in Canaan. Instead of gratitude, Israel burdened God with its sins. At first, God chose to ignore

> [17] Who leads out chariots and horsemen,
>   a powerful army,
> Till they lie prostrate together, never to rise,
>   snuffed out, quenched like a wick.
> [18] Remember not the events of the past,
>   the things of long ago consider not;
> [19] See, I am doing something new!
>   Now it springs forth, do you not perceive it?
> In the wilderness I make a way,
>   in the wasteland, rivers.
> [20] Wild beasts honor me,
>   jackals and ostriches,
> For I put water in the wilderness
>   and rivers in the wasteland
>   for my chosen people to drink,
> [21] The people whom I formed for myself,
>   that they might recount my praise.
>
> [22] Yet you did not call upon me, Jacob,
>   for you grew weary of me, Israel.
> [23] You did not bring me sheep for your burnt offerings,
>   nor honor me with your sacrifices.
> I did not exact from you the service of offerings,
>   nor weary you for frankincense.
> [24] You did not buy me sweet cane,
>   nor did you fill me with the fat of your sacrifices;
> Instead, you burdened me with your sins,
>   wearied me with your crimes.
> [25] It is I, I, who wipe out,
>   for my own sake, your offenses;
>   your sins I remember no more.
> [26] Would you have me remember, have us come to trial?
>   Speak up, prove your innocence!
>
> *continue*

Israel's sins, but its constant rebellion led God to remember the sins of all Israel—from those of Jacob to those of the present generation. God had no other choice but to abandon Israel. Still, the prophet suggests that Judah not focus on the past but on what God will do in the future.

Lesson Two

²⁷Your first father sinned;
  your spokesmen rebelled against me
²⁸Till I repudiated the holy princes,
  put Jacob under the ban,
  exposed Israel to scorn.

CHAPTER 44

¹Hear then, Jacob, my servant,
  Israel, whom I have chosen.
²Thus says the LORD who made you,
  your help, who formed you from the womb:
Do not fear, Jacob, my servant,
  Jeshurun, whom I have chosen.
³I will pour out water upon the thirsty ground,
  streams upon the dry land;
I will pour out my spirit upon your offspring,
  my blessing upon your descendants.
⁴They shall spring forth amid grass
  like poplars beside flowing waters.
⁵One shall say, "I am the LORD's,"
  another shall be named after Jacob,
And this one shall write on his hand, "The LORD's,"
  and receive the name Israel.

The True God and False Gods

⁶Thus says the LORD, Israel's king,
  its redeemer, the LORD of hosts:
I am the first, I am the last;
  there is no God but me.
⁷Who is like me? Let him stand up and declare,
  make it evident, and confront me with it.
Who of old announced future events?
  Let them foretell to us the things to come.
⁸Do not fear or be troubled.
Did I not announce it to you long ago?
  I declared it, and you are my witnesses.
Is there any God but me?
  There is no other Rock, I know of none!
⁹Those who fashion idols are all nothing;
  their precious works are of no avail.

continue

God has taken the initiative in empowering Israel as a witness. God will transform Israel and make it an effective witness though the outpouring of God's spirit into the dispirited exilic community. This community is God's *Jeshurun* (44:2; a Hebrew term translated as "darling" in the earlier NAB). The verbs of verses 4-5 point to some sort of an outward witness, not an inward transformation alone but something that people can see.

 The belief that **God knows us in the womb** even before our birth (44:2) is found elsewhere in the Old Testament. For example, when called to serve God as a prophet, Jeremiah is told that he had been dedicated to that work from the womb (Jer 1:5), and the psalmist proclaims that God "formed" his "inmost being" before birth and "knit" him in his mother's womb (Ps 139:13).

44:6-23 A parody on idol worship

The claims of the Lord's sovereignty seemed inflated to many people. After all, the Lord appeared unable to protect Judah from Babylon. At the very least, this must have led most of the prophet's contemporaries to view Israel's God as a second-rate deity. Certainly Marduk, Babylon's god, proved to be more powerful. Flying in the face of these attitudes, the prophet compares the Lord with other gods. The prophet begins by reminding people that the word of the Lord was spoken through the prophets who predicted the restoration of Jerusalem. That restoration is about to happen. This miracle will make the exiles God's witnesses before all peoples.

The prophet's comparison of Israel's God with the nations' gods continues with a parody on idol worship. The religion of ancient Israel was unique among the religions of the ancient Near East because it did not depict its patron deity in plastic form. Archaeologists have uncovered virtually no representations of male gods from the ancient Israelite period, though figurines depicting female deities have been found in surprising numbers. The torah prohibits the use of images of God several times: Exodus 20:4-5, 23; 34:17; Deuteronomy 4:15-18; 5:8; 27:15. The prophet plays on this special feature of Israelite religion to underscore the uniqueness of the Lord.

The prophet's basic point is that the gods of the nations are obviously unable to save because they are merely wooden or metal objects made by human beings. To make his point the prophet misrepresents ancient Near Eastern religious beliefs regarding images of the gods. The ancient peoples were not as naive as the prophet suggests. They believed that after an image was consecrated, the spirit of the god represented by the statue inhabited it. The purpose of the image was to help the god and its worshipers to focus their attention on each other. Some statues even had moving parts, allowing priests to give responses to inquiries made by worshipers. The veneration of icons and statues by Christians shows that images of the sacred have power, though people are aware they are human constructions.

The prophet insists that the reality of the Lord is not manifested through a fabricated image but through real people, who are going to make their way from the land of their exile back to their ancestral homeland. Forgiveness of sins and healing of memories equip Judah to be God's witness. Judah serves a God who forgives sins so that it can look to its past without despair and its future with hope. Judah is to regard its past infidelity like the dew that forms in the mornings of the dry season. It dissipates as soon as the sun rises above the horizon. So God's forgiveness makes Judah's sins just as insubstantial. It is not a statue that is the image of the divine but a living people whom God has redeemed. The calling of Judah is to be the living representation of the Lord. Its singing and rejoicing at the prospect of its impending return ought to stimulate nature to join in the praise of God.

The book of Revelation quotes verse 6, putting the words that the prophet attributes to God on the lips of the risen Jesus (Rev 1:8, 17).

> They are their witnesses:
>   they see nothing, know nothing,
>   and so they are put to shame.
> [10]Who would fashion a god or cast an idol,
>   that is of no use?
> [11]Look, all its company will be shamed;
>   they are artisans, mere human beings!
> They all assemble and stand there,
>   only to cower in shame.
> [12]The ironsmith fashions a likeness,
>   he works it over the coals,
> Shaping it with hammers,
>   working it with his strong arm.
> With hunger his strength wanes,
>   without water, he grows faint.
> [13]The woodworker stretches a line,
>   and marks out a shape with a stylus.
> He shapes it with scraping tools,
>   with a compass measures it off,
> Making it the copy of a man,
>   human display, enthroned in a shrine.
> [14]He goes out to cut down cedars,
>   takes a holm tree or an oak.
> He picks out for himself trees of the forest,
>   plants a fir, and the rain makes it grow.
> [15]It is used for fuel:
>   with some of the wood he warms himself,
>   makes a fire and bakes bread.
> Yet he makes a god and worships it,
>   turns it into an idol and adores it!
> [16]Half of it he burns in the fire,
>   on its embers he roasts meat;
>   he eats the roast and is full.
> He warms himself and says, "Ah!
>   I am warm! I see the flames!"
> [17]The rest of it he makes into a god,
>   an image to worship and adore.
> He prays to it and says,
>   "Help me! You are my god!"
> [18]They do not know, do not understand;
>   their eyes are too clouded to see,
>   their minds, to perceive.
> [19]He does not think clearly;
>   he lacks the wit and knowledge to say,
>
> *continue*

> "Half the wood I burned in the fire,
>   on its embers I baked bread,
>   I roasted meat and ate.
> Shall I turn the rest into an abomination?
>   Shall I worship a block of wood?"
> ²⁰He is chasing ashes!
> A deluded mind has led him astray;
>   He cannot save himself,
>   does not say, "This thing in my right
>   hand—is it not a fraud?"
>
> ²¹Remember these things, Jacob,
>   Israel, for you are my servant!
> I formed you, a servant to me;
>   Israel, you shall never be forgotten by me:
> ²²I have brushed away your offenses like a
>   cloud,
>   your sins like a mist;
>   return to me, for I have redeemed you.
>
> ²³Raise a glad cry, you heavens—the LORD
>   has acted!
> Shout, you depths of the earth.
> Break forth, mountains, into song,
>   forest, with all your trees.
> For the LORD has redeemed Jacob,
>   shows his glory through Israel.
>
> **Cyrus, Anointed of the Lord,
> Agent of Israel's Liberation**
>
> ²⁴Thus says the LORD, your redeemer,
>   who formed you from the womb:
> I am the LORD, who made all things,
>   who alone stretched out the heavens,
>   I spread out the earth by myself.
>
> *continue*

44:24–45:13 God's anointed king

Though the prophet has been speaking about the liberation of Jerusalem as a sovereign act of the Lord, he knows that the actual working out of the divine plan will happen through a human instrument. Abraham, Moses, Joshua, David, and the prophets have all served as the divinely chosen means by which God's will for Israel achieved its ends. Now the prophet is ready to identify the person whom he knows to be the one to effect the newest act of liberation: the redemption of Jerusalem's exiles. The prophet makes a surprising and unexpected identification to say the least.

The prophet begins by repeating the unprecedented nature of what God is about to do. Babylon's diviners did not foresee it. The king's advisors did not even consider the possibility. But it is true that Judah is going to be restored. Its cities—Jerusalem in particular—are going to be rebuilt and repopulated. But who is going to accomplish all this? The surprising answer is Cyrus, the king of Persia. Though the prophet hinted at this earlier (41:2, 25), here he does not use veiled references but makes an explicit identification. In this passage, the prophet mentions Cyrus by name twice (44:28; 45:1) and refers to him with a personal pronoun one more time (45:13).

What is even more surprising, the prophet calls Cyrus the Lord's "messiah" (anointed)—a title that was given to Israel's kings (1 Sam 2:10; 12:3; 2 Sam 23:1; Ps 2:2; 20:7; 132:17). In the book of Isaiah, the term does not have the eschatological connotations that it acquired later. Still, using it to speak of a non-Israelite king is unprecedented. Apparently, the prophet's notion of Jerusalem's liberation did not include the restoration of Judah's native dynasty. God will use Cyrus to free the exiles and enthrone him as king to free the exiles.

Not all the prophet's contemporaries welcomed this message, but he insists that the choice of Cyrus is God's. The only woe oracle that appears in the fourth section of the book (45:8-13) is directed at those who cannot accept the prophet's word about Cyrus. Without the restoration of Judah's native dynasty, there will be no restored Judahite state. By naming Cyrus as God's messiah, the prophet appears to accept a continuing subordinate role for Judah in the political sphere. Though the exiles will be free to return to their land, Judah will remain subject to the Persian king. Apparently, some of the exiles expected that any restoration of Judah would involve the restoration of the Davidic dynasty and Judahite national state.

Another institution of preexilic Israel that apparently does not have a significant place in the prophet's vision of Jerusalem's restoration is the temple. This is the only time the fourth section of the book of Isaiah mentions the temple (44:28). It follows the description of God's victory over chaotic forces represented by the waters of the seas and rivers (44:27). But victory over chaos and temple building are related activities. A temple makes the heavenly victory manifest to people on earth. Also, temple building was an expression of the king's claims to be divinely chosen. In fact, the decree of Cyrus that allows the exiles to return to Jerusalem states that God chose Cyrus to rebuild the temple of Jerusalem (2 Chr 36:22-23; Ezra 1:2-4).

God's choice of Cyrus as messiah makes it clear that the liberation of Jerusalem does not mean a return to the status quo of Judah's monarchic period. The prophet proclaims that God is about to do something entirely new. The miraculous liberation of Jerusalem will serve to broaden the horizons of Judah's concept of God.

> ²⁵I bring to nought the omens of babblers,
>   make fools of diviners,
> Turn back the wise
>   and make their knowledge foolish.
> ²⁶I confirm the words of my servant,
>   carry out the plan my messengers announce.
> I say to Jerusalem, Be inhabited!
>   To the cities of Judah, Be rebuilt!
>   I will raise up their ruins.
> ²⁷I say to the deep, Be dry!
>   I will dry up your rivers.
> ²⁸I say of Cyrus, My shepherd!
>   He carries out my every wish,
> Saying of Jerusalem, "Let it be rebuilt,"
>   and of the temple, "Lay its foundations."
>
> **CHAPTER 45**
>
> ¹Thus says the LORD to his anointed, Cyrus,
>   whose right hand I grasp,
> Subduing nations before him,
>   stripping kings of their strength,
>
> *continue*

Illustration of a carving of Cyrus the Great found in the capital city of Pasargadae

 What do we know about Cyrus?

Cyrus II, also known as Cyrus the Great, is considered the founder of the Persian Empire (see map on p. 11), which he ruled from 558–530 B.C. Originally a client-king of the Medes, shortly after ascending the throne Cyrus was able to consolidate the nomadic tribes he governed and revolt against his Median overlords. His successful rebellion was followed by a series of conquests, first of Lydia and then Babylon. It was Cyrus who would fulfill the oracle that Daniel interpreted for King Belshazzar, predicting that Babylon would be "divided and given to the Medes and Persians" (Dan 5:28). Isaiah's identification of Cyrus as God's "shepherd" (44:28) points to his work as God's agent in the repatriation of Israel and does so with a play on the king's name, for Cyrus is derived from the Persian *kurash*, which means "shepherd."

In 1879 a cylinder of baked clay from the sixth century B.C. was discovered during an archeological excavation of Babylon. The inscription on the cylinder contains a description of Cyrus's victory over Babylon and his policy of allowing Babylonian captives to return to their homelands and rebuild their sacred places.

Opening doors before him,
    leaving the gates unbarred:
²I will go before you
    and level the mountains;
Bronze doors I will shatter,
    iron bars I will snap.
³I will give you treasures of darkness,
    riches hidden away,
That you may know I am the Lord,
    the God of Israel, who calls you by name.

⁴For the sake of Jacob, my servant,
    of Israel my chosen one,
I have called you by name,
    giving you a title, though you do not know me.
⁵I am the Lord, there is no other,
    there is no God besides me.
It is I who arm you, though you do not know me,
    ⁶so that all may know, from the rising of the sun
    to its setting, that there is none besides me.
I am the Lord, there is no other.
    ⁷I form the light, and create the darkness,
I make weal and create woe;
    I, the Lord, do all these things.
⁸Let justice descend, you heavens, like dew from above,
    like gentle rain let the clouds drop it down.
Let the earth open and salvation bud forth;
    let righteousness spring up with them!
    I, the Lord, have created this.
⁹Woe to anyone who contends with their Maker;
    a potsherd among potsherds of the earth!
Shall the clay say to the potter, "What are you doing?"
    or, "What you are making has no handles"?
¹⁰Woe to anyone who asks a father, "What are you begetting?"
    or a woman, "What are you giving birth to?"

¹¹Thus says the Lord,
    the Holy One of Israel, his maker:
Do you question me about my children,
    tell me how to treat the work of my hands?
¹²It was I who made the earth
    and created the people upon it;
It was my hands that stretched out the heavens;
    I gave the order to all their host.
¹³It was I who stirred him up for justice;
    all his ways I make level.
He shall rebuild my city
    and let my exiles go free
Without price or payment,
    says the Lord of hosts.

¹⁴Thus says the Lord:
The earnings of Egypt, the gain of Ethiopia,
    and the Sabeans, tall of stature,
Shall come over to you and belong to you;
    they shall follow you, coming in chains.
Before you they shall bow down,
    saying in prayer:
"With you alone is God; and there is none other,
    no other god!
¹⁵Truly with you God is hidden,
    the God of Israel, the savior!
¹⁶They are put to shame and disgrace, all of them;
    they go in disgrace who carve images.
¹⁷Israel has been saved by the Lord,
    saved forever!
You shall never be put to shame or disgrace in any future age."

¹⁸For thus says the Lord,
The creator of the heavens,
    who is God,
The designer and maker of the earth
    who established it,
Not as an empty waste did he create it,
    but designing it to be lived in:
I am the Lord, and there is no other.
¹⁹I have not spoken in secret
    from some place in the land of darkness,

continue

45:14-25 God and the nations

Another important element of the prophet's vision of Jerusalem's future involves the nations. Here too the prophet proclaims something new. The previous sections of the book of Isaiah presented the nations as enemies of Judah bent on its destruction. Though they were instruments of divine judgment, the nations often went beyond their mandate and would themselves experience severe judgment for their excesses. Here the prophet has the nations recognize the Lord's role in the fall of Babylon, the rise of Persia, and the liberation of Jerusalem. By defeating Judah, the nations served God's purposes without knowing it, but this new act of God would make it possible for them to recognize Israel's God as the only God.

The nations confess that it is clear that the Lord alone is God and God's intentions for Judah are clear, whereas once they were hidden. God is "hidden" since God has been with Judah in exile, but now that exile is about to end in a glorious and miraculous way. The peoples of exotic lands will leave their countries in order to come to Jerusalem so that they might see the great victory that God has given to Judah, a victory which has meant defeat for those nations that were threats to Judah's existence.

God asserts that God's intentions have always been clear in the creation of the world and through the demand for justice. God's word was not uttered in some secret place but openly. A similar point is made in the book of Acts. During the controversy regarding the obligation of Gentile converts to Christianity to observe the torah, James notes that the Mosaic law had been proclaimed in every city since Moses "has been read in the synagogues every sabbath" (Acts 15:21). Paul too asserts that what the law requires is written on the hearts of the Gentiles (Rom 2:15). Still, the notion that Israel's God is a "hidden" God does help people to recognize the tentativeness of their insights into God's presence and action in the world. While believers look forward to the day of God's final victory over the powers of evil, they recognize that in the meantime it is not always easy to see God's purposes being fulfilled.

I have not said to the descendants of Jacob,
   "Look for me in an empty waste."
I, the Lord, promise justice,
   I declare what is right.

²⁰Come and assemble, gather together,
   you fugitives from among the nations!
They are without knowledge who bear
      wooden idols
   and pray to gods that cannot save.
²¹Come close and declare;
   let them take counsel together:
Who announced this from the beginning,
   declared it from of old?
Was it not I, the Lord,
   besides whom there is no other God?
   There is no just and saving God but me.

²²Turn to me and be safe,
   all you ends of the earth,
   for I am God; there is no other!
²³By myself I swear,
   uttering my just decree,
   a word that will not return:
To me every knee shall bend;
   by me every tongue shall swear,
²⁴Saying, "Only in the Lord
   are just deeds and power.
Before him in shame shall come
   all who vent their anger against him.
²⁵In the Lord all the descendants of Israel
   shall have vindication and glory."

CHAPTER 46

The Gods of Babylon

¹Bel bows down, Nebo stoops,
   their idols set upon beasts and cattle;
They must be borne upon shoulders,
   a load for weary animals.
²They stoop and bow down together;
   unable to deliver those who bear them,
   they too go into captivity.

³Hear me, O house of Jacob,
   all the remnant of the house of Israel,

continue

> My burden from the womb,
>   whom I have carried since birth.
> ⁴Even to your old age I am he,
>   even when your hair is gray I will carry you;
> I have done this, and I will lift you up,
>   I will carry you to safety.
>
> ⁵To whom would you liken me as an equal,
>   compare me, as though we were alike?
> ⁶There are those who pour out gold from a purse
>   and weigh out silver on the scales;
> They hire a goldsmith to make it into a god
>   before which they bow down in worship.
> ⁷They lift it to their shoulders to carry;
>   when they set it down, it stays,
>   and does not move from the place.
> They cry out to it, but it cannot answer;
>   it delivers no one from distress.
> ⁸Remember this and be firm,
>   take it to heart, you rebels;
> ⁹remember the former things, those long ago:
> I am God, there is no other;
>   I am God, there is none like me.
> ¹⁰At the beginning I declare the outcome;
>   from of old, things not yet done.
> I say that my plan shall stand,
>   I accomplish my every desire.
> ¹¹I summon from the east a bird of prey,
>   from a distant land, one to carry out my plan.
> Yes, I have spoken, I will accomplish it;
>   I have planned it, and I will do it.
> ¹²Listen to me, you fainthearted,
>   far from the victory of justice:
> ¹³I am bringing on that victory, it is not far off,
>   my salvation shall not tarry;
> I will put salvation within Zion,
>   give to Israel my glory.

The prophet's vision has the nations joining Judah in acknowledging the Lord as the only God. Jerusalem's liberation, when it did come, did not have the effect on the nations that the prophet anticipated. But 45:23b-24a is cited in both Romans 14:11 and Philippians 2:10-11 for Paul believed that the prophet's vision would find its fulfillment in Jesus and the church.

46:1-13 Salvation in Zion

This passage contrasts Babylon and its gods, Bel and Nebo, with Zion and its God. It opens with Bel and Nebo being led away from Babylon in captivity and ends with the affirmation that God "will put salvation within Zion" (46:13).

Bel was a title given to Marduk, Babylon's patron deity. Nebo was the son of Marduk, whose temple was across the Euphrates from Babylon. These gods had to be carried by their worshipers while the Lord "carr[ies]" the people of Judah. In drawing this contrast, the prophet expected that the Persians would follow usual practice by carrying off the images of the gods of the conquered cities, but Cyrus had a different policy. He was as tolerant toward the Babylonians and their religion as he was toward the people of Judah. He tried to show himself to the Babylonians as Marduk's chosen instrument to insure the proper service of that god.

The prophet asserts that the Lord's dominion is not like that of the other gods who cannot save because they are manufactured images and nothing more. This passage again ridicules the worship of other gods in order to eliminate rival claimants for Judah's loyalty. The prophet calls skeptics from both Judah and the nations to remember what God has done. Cyrus is the destroyer of Babylon's military power. The destruction of Babylon and the flight of its helpless gods send a clear message to Israel: do not keep yourselves distant from the shrine of the Lord in Zion. The doubters need to be told that the conquest of Babylon by Cyrus, though apparently unrelated to Judah's destiny, was actually an act of God to restore the people of Judah to Jerusalem. The people then are to attend to the fulfillment of prophecy and the exclusive claims of the Lord as manifest through the rise of Cyrus.

EXPLORING LESSON TWO

1. a) How does the prophet use the exodus event as a kind of template for God's new action on behalf of Israel (43:16-21)?

   b) How is this same exodus pattern employed in the New Testament? (See examples in Luke 9:28-31; John 3:14-15; 6:32-35; Col 1:13-14.)

2. How has God offered you comfort and assurance when you felt you were unlovable or abandoned (44:2)?

3. Water, especially in a barren landscape, is symbolic of renewal, life, and even prosperity (44:3). In what ways is the symbolic power of water continued in Christian practice? (See Acts 8:37-38; Titus 3:4-7.)

Lesson Two

4. a) What evidence is offered to illustrate that false idols do not have the power that God possesses (44:9, 18-19)? (See also 45:16-17; Deut 4:28; Ps 115:4-8.)

b) In contrast, how is Israel's God portrayed (44:21)?

5. Babylon's destruction of Jerusalem and the temple was historically and spiritually significant. (See 2 Kgs 24:10-17; Lam 1:1-8.) How do you think the message of 44:26-28 would have sounded to the ears of those about to be released from exile?

6. Why was it significant that God through Isaiah identifies Cyrus as "My shepherd" (44:28) and "anointed" (45:1)?

7. What is the purpose of God's rebuke in 45:9-13?

Lesson Two

8. Verses 15 and 19 of chapter 45 almost seem to contradict each other. How have you experienced both the hiddenness and the boldness of God in your life?

_____

_____

_____

_____

_____

9. Although 46:1-2 predicts that Babylon will suffer the fate of most peoples conquered in battle, what does the commentary indicate actually happened after Persia conquered Babylon?

_____

_____

_____

_____

_____

10. Variations of God's declaration "I am the Lord" are found throughout this portion of the book of Isaiah (43:3, 11-12, 15; 44:24; 45:5-6, 18, 22; 46:9). This divine title highlights God's authority, power, and influence. How do you experience God as Lord in your life?

_____

_____

_____

_____

_____

CLOSING PRAYER

Prayer

Thus says the Lord, Israel's king,
  its redeemer, the Lord of hosts:
I am the first, I am the last;
  there is no God but me. (Isa 44:6)

Preserve us, Lord, from all that would separate us from your love. Give us the wisdom to see that the things that distract us or lead us away from you are but idols, seeking to replace you in our hearts. Let us begin this day to center our lives on you alone, especially by . . .

LESSON THREE

Isaiah 47–50

Begin your personal study and group discussion with a simple and sincere prayer such as:

Prayer

Lord God, as we continue our study of Isaiah, may our hearts remain open to the prophet's proclamation of your boundless love for your people. Inspire us with your Spirit so we may always be moved to seek you and to serve one another.

Read the Bible text of Isaiah 47–50 found in the outside columns of pages 46–54, highlighting what stands out to you.

Read the accompanying commentary to add to your understanding.

Respond to the questions on pages 55–57, Exploring Lesson Three.

The Closing Prayer on page 58 is for your personal use and may be used at the end of group discussion.

Lesson Three

CHAPTER 47

The Fall of Babylon

¹Come down, sit in the dust,
    virgin daughter Babylon;
Sit on the ground, dethroned,
    daughter of the Chaldeans.
No longer shall you be called
    dainty and delicate.
²Take the millstone and grind flour,
    remove your veil;
Strip off your skirt, bare your legs,
    cross through the streams.
³Your nakedness shall be uncovered,
    and your shame be seen;
I will take vengeance,
    I will yield to no entreaty,
        says ⁴our redeemer,
Whose name is the LORD of hosts,
    the Holy One of Israel.

⁵Go into darkness and sit in silence,
    daughter of the Chaldeans,
No longer shall you be called
    sovereign mistress of kingdoms.
⁶Angry at my people,
    I profaned my heritage
And gave them into your power;
    but you showed them no mercy;
Upon the aged
    you laid a very heavy yoke.
⁷You said, "I shall remain always,
    a sovereign mistress forever!"
You did not take these things to heart,
    but disregarded their outcome.
⁸Now hear this, voluptuous one,
    enthroned securely,
Saying in your heart,
    "I, and no one else!
I shall never be a widow,
    bereft of my children"—
⁹Both these things shall come to you
    suddenly, in a single day:
Complete bereavement and widowhood
    shall come upon you

continue

47:1-15 Against Babylon

The only way for the liberation of Jerusalem to proceed is for Babylon to fall. The prophet taunts Babylon by asserting that God will strip it of all prerogatives as a royal city. He declares that this pampered daughter of the Chaldeans, who provided the neo-Babylonian empire with its leadership, will do the work of slaves such as grinding grain into meal. Once an untouchable queen, she will be devastated and subject to sexual harassment like any commoner (compare Hos 2:9-12; Jer 13:20-27). The Lord empowered Babylon to conquer Judah because of the latter's infidelity—not because of Babylon's virtue or because of its military power. Babylon mistook this temporary mission as conferring permanent, privileged status. It thought itself exempt from military defeat and political impotence. It will experience both.

The skills of Babylon's priests and diviners cannot save its empire. Babylon had an international reputation for the skills of its sages and diviners. In the face of the Lord's judgment they are impotent. There are no rituals or charms that can forestall the judgment that awaits Babylon. It is inevitable. Babylon's fall will be quick and spectacular, like fire that consumes dry stubble (47:14). Allies and vassals will leave Babylon to face its fate alone. The book of Revelation imitates the prophet when it taunts

Rome, whose fall its author considered inevitable (Rev 17–18). Like Babylon, Rome was the capital of a great empire. Still, both Babylon and Rome were transformed by the power of God. Neither was destroyed, but Babylon became a great center of Jewish learning and Rome became the capital of the Christian world. The visions of both prophets Isaiah and John were fulfilled beyond their expectations.

 Cities are commonly personified as women in the Old Testament, and villages around a city are often called "daughters." Babylon is described as a virgin and daughter (47:1), mother and widow (47:8-9), and queen (47:5). Jerusalem is described in similar terms: virgin (37:22), bride (62:5), wife (54:5-6), widow (54:4), and mother (66:7-13).

48:1-22 The power of God's word

The prophet's task is to persuade the exiles that his view of Jerusalem's liberation is not just a flight of fancy but the word of God that is going to be fulfilled and soon. What kept people from accepting the prophet's message was their experience—the harsh realities of their lives in exile. To believe that the Lord, the patron deity of a nation and dynasty that no longer existed, was controlling world events strained the people's credulity. Judah was no longer even a minor player on the stage in the ancient Near East. Babylon, whose material culture, military might, and political power far outstripped that of Judah's best days, could not possibly be threatened by any message from the Lord, no matter how convinced the prophet may be.

In this chapter the prophet is venting his frustration at the exiles' unenthusiastic response to his message. He tries to persuade people that the message he is delivering is the word of God, a word that will find fulfillment. There are two parts in this unit: verses 1-11 and verses 12-21. The first embodies a theory of the connection between God's word and God's deeds, and the second applies this theory to the exilic situation and the rise of Cyrus.

Despite your many sorceries
  and the full power of your spells;
¹⁰Secure in your wickedness,
  you said, "No one sees me."
Your wisdom and your knowledge
  led you astray,
And you said in your heart,
  "I, and no one else!"
¹¹But upon you shall come an evil
  you will not be able to charm away;
Upon you shall fall a disaster
  you cannot ward off.
Upon you shall suddenly come
  a ruin you cannot imagine.

¹²Keep on with your spells
  and your many sorceries,
  at which you toiled from your youth.
Perhaps you can prevail,
  perhaps you can strike terror!
¹³You wore yourself out with so many
    consultations!
  Let the astrologers stand forth to save you,
The stargazers who forecast at each new moon
  what would happen to you.
¹⁴See, they are like stubble,
  fire consumes them;
They cannot deliver themselves
  from the spreading flames.
This is no warming ember,
  no fire to sit before!
¹⁵Thus do your wizards serve you
  with whom you have toiled from your
    youth;
They wander their separate ways,
  with none to save you.

CHAPTER 48

Exhortations to the Exiles

¹Hear this, house of Jacob
  called by the name Israel,
  sprung from the stock of Judah,
You who swear by the name of the Lord
  and invoke the God of Israel
  without sincerity, without justice,

continue

²Though you are named after the holy city
 and rely on the God of Israel,
 whose name is the Lord of hosts.
³Things of the past I declared long ago,
 they went forth from my mouth, I announced them;
 then suddenly I took action and they came to be.
⁴Because I know that you are stubborn
 and that your neck is an iron sinew
 and your forehead bronze,
⁵I declared them to you of old;
 before they took place I informed you,
That you might not say, "My idol did them,
 my statue, my molten image commanded them."
⁶Now that you have heard, look at all this;
 must you not admit it?
From now on I announce new things to you,
 hidden events you never knew.
⁷Now, not from of old, they are created,
 before today you did not hear of them,
 so that you cannot claim, "I have known them."
⁸You never heard, you never knew,
 they never reached your ears beforehand.
Yes, I know you are utterly treacherous,
 a rebel you were named from the womb.
⁹For the sake of my name I restrain my anger,
 for the sake of my renown I hold it back from you,
 lest I destroy you.
¹⁰See, I refined you, but not like silver;
 I tested you in the furnace of affliction.
¹¹For my sake, for my own sake, I do this;
 why should my name be profaned?
 My glory I will not give to another.
¹²Listen to me, Jacob,
 Israel, whom I called!
I, it is I who am the first,
 and am I the last.
¹³Yes, my hand laid the foundations of the earth;

continue

The prophet begins by showing that there is a connection between God's word and Israel's experience, as is clear from Israel's past. The prophet also criticizes a shallow religion that saw Israel's security in its cult and believed that Israel's God had no moral will. He asserts that the word must precede God's actions in Judah's life because of its stubbornness in the past. Judah will know that the Lord is responsible once the word is fulfilled. Unfortunately, the people have shown a tendency to attribute the course of events to some agent other than the Lord. The preexilic prophets contain ample number of threats of judgment on moral grounds, and it was in these that the revealing word of the Lord was contained. The exiles preferred to explain their misfortunes by something other than the moral and religious breakdown of which the prophets spoke.

There is no great act of God without a predictive word to clarify its significance. Judah thinks that it knows who God is and how God acts. It will deny the divine origin of anything that is contrary to its concept of God and the biases connected with it. Of course, this is to be expected since Israel was rebellious from its very beginning. But the Lord is not governed by the conduct of Israel. Whether God judges or saves, the motivation is within God's inner being, i.e., God's name. God does not respond to emotional impulse like human beings. The Lord's work will proceed no matter what the popular reaction is.

 Concern for God's "name" and "renown" (48:9) is a common motivation for divine action in the Old Testament. Abraham uses concern for God's reputation for justice to convince God to spare Sodom if ten righteous people could be found in the city (Gen 18:32), and Moses uses a similar argument to convince God to spare the Israelites after they erected the golden calf (Exod 32:12-13). The psalms are rich in references to God acting in human affairs for the sake of God's name (Pss 23:3; 31:3; 79:9; 106:8; 109:21; 143:11).

In the second part of this passage (48:11-22), the prophet applies what he just said about the power of God's word to the situation that Judah faces. The prophet is providing the word and Cyrus is doing the deed. God chose Cyrus to act against Babylon and has guaranteed his success. The fall of Babylon has no significance apart from its manifestation of God's power.

The speaker of verse 16 is Cyrus, who acknowledges that he will conquer Babylon by the power of God's spirit. The messenger formula in the following verse introduces a statement that offers a perspective similar to that undergirding the book of Deuteronomy: if Israel will learn and observe God's teaching, this will guarantee Israel's prosperity, but the "commandments" in verse 18 probably refer to the prophet's words rather than stipulations of the torah. Israel's future is linked to obedience to the authoritative words of the prophet. Using a series of imperatives in verses 20-21, the prophet calls for a new exodus and a new passage through the desert. The prophet summons Israel to action. Verse 22 appears almost verbatim in 57:21. It is not related to the context here and seems to be a discordant note at the end of a text that shows progressive emotional intensity.

John of Patmos gives advice that is the same as that of the prophet. The book of Revelation calls Christians to depart from Rome (Rev 18:4), just as the prophet charges the exiles to leave Babylon (48:20). Believers are called to respond to God's word. They are not to remain passive recipients but active agents of that word. They are to leave behind all that has left them insensitive to the message of God's prophets. John also uses the prophet's epithets "first" and "last" to speak about Christ (48:12; Rev 1:17; 2:8; see also Isa 44:6).

49:1-6 Israel's mission

The prophet wishes to present his message of Jerusalem's liberation against the widest possible backdrop. It is essential that the exiles do not conceive of their release from captivity as making possible a return to the political, economic, social, and religious conditions of Judah

> my right hand spread out the heavens.
> When I summon them,
>   they stand forth at once.
>
> ¹⁴All of you assemble and listen:
>   Who among you declared these things?
> The one the LORD loves shall do his will
>   against Babylon and the offspring of Chaldea.
> ¹⁵I myself have spoken, I have summoned him,
>   I have brought him, and his way succeeds!
> ¹⁶Come near to me and hear this!
>   From the beginning I did not speak in secret;
> At the time it happens, I am there:
>   "Now the Lord GOD has sent me, and his spirit."
>
> ¹⁷Thus says the LORD, your redeemer,
>   the Holy One of Israel:
> I am the LORD, your God,
>   teaching you how to prevail,
>   leading you on the way you should go.
> ¹⁸If only you would attend to my commandments,
>   your peace would be like a river,
>   your vindication like the waves of the sea,
> ¹⁹Your descendants like the sand,
>   the offspring of your loins like its grains,
> Their name never cut off
>   or blotted out from my presence.
> ²⁰Go forth from Babylon, flee from Chaldea!
>   With shouts of joy declare this, announce it;
> Make it known to the ends of the earth,
>   Say: "The LORD has redeemed his servant Jacob.
> ²¹They did not thirst
>   when he led them through dry lands;
> Water from the rock he set flowing for them;
>   he cleft the rock, and waters welled forth."
>
> ²²There is no peace for the wicked,
>   says the LORD.
>
> *continue*

CHAPTER 49

The Servant of the Lord

¹Hear me, coastlands,
 listen, distant peoples.
Before birth the LORD called me,
 from my mother's womb he gave me my name.
²He made my mouth like a sharp-edged sword,
 concealed me, shielded by his hand.
He made me a sharpened arrow,
 in his quiver he hid me.
³He said to me, You are my servant,
 in you, Israel, I show my glory.

⁴Though I thought I had toiled in vain,
 for nothing and for naught spent my strength,
Yet my right is with the LORD,
 my recompense is with my God.
⁵For now the LORD has spoken
 who formed me as his servant from the womb,
That Jacob may be brought back to him
 and Israel gathered to him;
I am honored in the sight of the LORD,
 and my God is now my strength!
⁶It is too little, he says, for you to be my servant,
 to raise up the tribes of Jacob,
 and restore the survivors of Israel;
I will make you a light to the nations,
 that my salvation may reach to the ends of the earth.
⁷Thus says the LORD,
 the redeemer, the Holy One of Israel,
To the one despised, abhorred by the nations,
 the slave of rulers:
When kings see you, they shall stand up,
 and princes shall bow down
Because of the LORD who is faithful,
 the Holy One of Israel who has chosen you.

continue

before the fall of Jerusalem. Judah will have a future, but that future consists in bringing the word of God "to the ends of the earth" (49:6). It is for this reason that Israel was chosen as God's people (see Gen 12:3). Jerusalem's restoration will make it possible for the people to present a dramatic and authentic witness of God's power. Luke quotes verse 6 to show that God was controlling the events that led to the decision by Paul and Barnabas to preach to the Gentiles (Acts 13:47) and he sees the church fulfilling Israel's mission to proclaim the word of God "to the ends of the earth" (Acts 1:8).

 Isaiah's request that God make his mouth **"like a sharp-edged sword"** (49:2) contains a play on the Hebrew idiom referring to the edge of a sword as its "mouth." This is an apt description, given that the sword devours human life (Deut 32:42; 2 Sam 11:25). The ability of the sword to cut indicates speech that is sharp and forceful. Similar use is made of the sword as an image of the powerful word of God in several New Testament texts (Eph 6:17; Heb 4:12; Rev 2:16; 19:15).

49:7 The reaction of the nations

There will be a dramatic reversal of fortunes following Jerusalem's liberation. The miracle that God will work in and through Judah will be such that the only possible response will be for kings and princes to acknowledge the sovereignty of Israel's God. While this verse is a testament to the prophet's faith, it was not fulfilled in the way he expected. The restoration never achieved the goals that the prophet had for it. This led to further reflection on and a reinterpretation of the prophet's message. One outcome of this reinterpretation was the appropriation of the book of Isaiah by the writers of the New Testament. They believed that the prophet's words finally found their fulfillment in Jesus and the gospel.

Lesson Three

49:8-26 The reaction of the exiles

While the prophet foresees that princes and kings will prostrate themselves before Judah's God when they witness the fulfillment of God's word, the reaction of God's people to that word is lamentation. The prophet characterizes the days during which he spoke in the name of God as "a time of favor" (49:8). This was the time that the people of Judah were praying for. God was answering their prayers and would lead them back to Zion. The word that God has for the exiles is "Come out!" (49:9). The return to Jerusalem will be less like a wearisome trek and more like a procession led by God, who will guide the people as a shepherd. Judahite exiles from all over the world, not just Babylon, will stream toward their ancient homeland (49:12: Syene is the modern Aswan in Upper Egypt where there was a Jewish colony).

 Although **tattooing** was a forbidden practice for the Israelites (Lev 19:28), the prohibition likely referred specifically to marks made on the body as a sign of dedication to a foreign deity. The reference to "walls" in Isaiah 49:16 ("your walls are ever before me") has suggested to some scholars that what is engraved on God's hands is a blueprint for the reconstruction of Jerusalem.

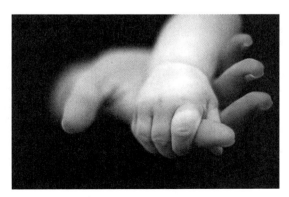

"Can a mother forget . . . the child of her womb? . . . See, upon the palms of my hands I have engraved you." (49:15-16)

The Liberation and Restoration of Zion

⁸Thus says the LORD:
In a time of favor I answer you,
   on the day of salvation I help you;
I form you and set you
   as a covenant for the people,
To restore the land
   and allot the devastated heritages,
⁹To say to the prisoners: Come out!
   To those in darkness: Show yourselves!
Along the roadways they shall find pasture,
   on every barren height shall their pastures be.
¹⁰They shall not hunger or thirst;
   nor shall scorching wind or sun strike them;
For he who pities them leads them
   and guides them beside springs of water.
¹¹I will turn all my mountains into roadway,
   and make my highways level.
¹²See, these shall come from afar:
   some from the north and the west,
   others from the land of Syene.

¹³Sing out, heavens, and rejoice, earth,
   break forth into song, you mountains,
For the LORD comforts his people
   and shows mercy to his afflicted.

¹⁴But Zion said, "The LORD has forsaken me;
   my Lord has forgotten me."
¹⁵Can a mother forget her infant,
   be without tenderness for the child of her womb?
Even should she forget,
   I will never forget you.
¹⁶See, upon the palms of my hands I have engraved you;
   your walls are ever before me.
¹⁷Your children hasten—
   your levelers, your destroyers
   go forth from you;
¹⁸Look about and see,
   they are all gathering and coming to you.

continue

> As I live—oracle of the LORD—
>   you shall don them as jewels,
>   bedeck yourself like a bride.
>
> ¹⁹Though you were waste and desolate,
>   a land of ruins,
> Now you shall be too narrow for your
>   inhabitants,
>   while those who swallowed you up will be
>   far away.
> ²⁰The children of whom you were bereft
>   shall yet say in your hearing,
> "This place is too narrow for me,
>   make room for me to live in."
> ²¹You shall ask yourself:
> "Who has borne me these,
>   when I was bereft and barren?
> Exiled and repudiated,
>   who has reared them?
> I was left all alone;
>   where then do these come from?"
> ²²Thus says the Lord GOD:
> See, I will lift up my hand to the nations,
>   and to the peoples raise my signal;
> They shall bring your sons in their arms,
>   your daughters shall be carried on their
>   shoulders.
> ²³Kings shall be your guardians,
>   their princesses your nursemaids;
> Face to the ground, they shall bow down
>   before you
>   and lick the dust at your feet.
> Then you shall know that I am the LORD,
>   none who hope in me shall be ashamed.
> ²⁴Can plunder be taken from a warrior,
>   or captives rescued from a tyrant?
> ²⁵Thus says the LORD:
> Yes, captives can be taken from a warrior,
>   and plunder rescued from a tyrant;
> Those who oppose you I will oppose,
>   and your sons I will save.
> ²⁶I will make your oppressors eat their own
>   flesh,
>   and they shall be drunk with their own
>   blood
>
> *continue*

Inanimate nature recognizes Judah's restoration for what it is: a miraculous demonstration of God's power. It responds with uninhibited joy. The liberation of Jerusalem is no mere political event. The cosmos is caught up in this redemptive act of God that restores the people of Judah not only to their homeland but especially to their unique relationship with God. The people have suffered because of their infidelity, but God's compassion will not allow God's justice to have its full effect on Israel. Judgment was not to be God's last word. The prophet sees the people's redemption on the horizon. Nature too sees this and rejoices.

How do the exiles react to the momentous events in which they are caught up? How do they respond to the prophet's words of hope? Unlike the heavens and the earth, which recognize the significance of God's action, the people of Judah utter words of disbelief. The exiles consider the prophet's message unrealistic—too good to be true. Perhaps they considered them the product of an overwrought religious personality.

To counter the exiles' disbelief, the prophet uses a very poignant metaphor. He asserts that God's love for the people of Judah exceeds that of a nursing mother for her child. While some biblical metaphors can be difficult to understand, the image in verse 15 is impossible to misinterpret. It is difficult to find a more touching image of God's love anywhere else in the Bible. This image underscores the unbreakable bond between God and Israel. While this bond did not exempt Israel from experiencing divine judgment for its infidelity, God's commitment to Israel remains secure. The phrase in verse 16a ("See, upon the palms of my hands I have engraved you . . . ") may refer to tattooing, another image of the permanency of God's commitment to Israel. The prophet promises that Jerusalem will be rebuilt and repopulated. He then returns to a familiar motif: the reversal of the fortunes of Judah and Babylon leading all peoples to recognize that the Lord's power saved Judah.

Paul cited 49:8 to urge the people of Corinth to respond to God's grace at work in them (see

2 Cor 6:2). Like the prophet, Paul believed that apart from the believers' response the transforming power of God's word would not have concrete effect.

 The grisly promise that God will make Israel's oppressors **"eat their own flesh"** (49:26) is a reminder of the extremes to which besieged populations could be driven in antiquity. Israel's experience of such horrific circumstances is historically attested by both biblical and non-biblical sources (see, for example, 2 Kgs 6:26-29 and Josephus, *Jewish Wars*: 6.3.4). Another way of reading this verse is to see it as a rhetorical exaggeration meant to emphasize that God's victory over Israel's enemies will be complete.

50:1-3 The purpose of the exiles

To counter the exiles' lack of hope regarding their future, the prophet assures them that the purpose of the exile was not to end Jerusalem's relationship with God but to discipline its people. Both Hosea and Jeremiah use the metaphor of divorce (Hos 2:4; Jer 3:1, 8) to speak about the consequences that Israel will have to pay for its infidelity, but the prophet rejects this comparison. He maintains that there was no divorce between Jerusalem ("your mother") and God since no bill of divorce was given (see Deut 24:1-4). He also asserts that, despite appearances, the people were not sold into slavery, since that would imply that God needed to sell Israel to settle debts. God has no creditors. What happened to the people of Judah happened because they did not recognize the power of their God, who alone overcame the mighty waters to bring order out of chaos. God's power will now liberate Jerusalem from its exile.

50:4-11 Light and darkness

The prophet identifies himself with all those whom God sent to bring light to those who preferred to live in darkness. This passage

as though with new wine.
All flesh shall know
  that I, the LORD, am your savior,
  your redeemer, the Mighty One of Jacob.

CHAPTER 50

Salvation Through the Lord's Servant

¹Thus says the LORD:
Where is the bill of divorce
  with which I dismissed your mother?
Or to which of my creditors
  have I sold you?
It was for your sins you were sold,
  for your rebellions your mother was
    dismissed.

²Why was no one there when I came?
  Why did no one answer when I called?
Is my hand too short to ransom?
  Have I not the strength to deliver?
See, with my rebuke I dry up the sea,
  I turn rivers into wilderness;
Their fish rot for lack of water,
  and die of thirst.
³I clothe the heavens in black,
  and make sackcloth their covering.

⁴The Lord GOD has given me
  a well-trained tongue,
That I might know how to answer the weary
  a word that will waken them.
Morning after morning
  he wakens my ear to hear as disciples do;
⁵The Lord GOD opened my ear;
  I did not refuse,
  did not turn away.
⁶I gave my back to those who beat me,
  my cheeks to those who tore out my beard;
My face I did not hide
  from insults and spitting.

⁷The Lord GOD is my help,
  therefore I am not disgraced;
Therefore I have set my face like flint,
  knowing that I shall not be put to shame.

continue

> ⁸He who declares my innocence is near.
>   Who will oppose me?
>   Let us appear together.
> Who will dispute my right?
>   Let them confront me.
> ⁹See, the Lord GOD is my help;
>   who will declare me guilty?
> See, they will all wear out like a garment,
>   consumed by moths.
> ¹⁰Who among you fears the LORD,
>   heeds his servant's voice?
> Whoever walk in darkness,
>   without any light,
> Yet trust in the name of the LORD
>   and rely upon their God!
> ¹¹All you who kindle flames
>   and set flares alight,
> Walk by the light of your own fire
>   and by the flares you have burnt!
> This is your fate from my hand:
>   you shall lie down in a place of torment.

is reminiscent of a thanksgiving psalm (e.g., Ps 34) with its description of distress and the affirmation that God saved the prophet. In the midst of humiliating treatment, the prophet asserts that God was with him, so that in the end he will be vindicated. The prophet then turns to his audience and tells them that they may enjoy the same divine protection. The prophet agrees that he walks in the darkness of the exile, but he urges his audience to trust in God so that they might join him in the light. This passage has been listed among the "Servant Songs," though the word "servant" does not appear here.

Lesson Three

EXPLORING LESSON THREE

1. Isaiah is filled with imagery. After reading through the description of the fall of Babylon (47:1-15), which of the images used by the prophet to describe Babylon's doom is most interesting to you? Why?

2. In what ways has the church (the universal church or your local community) been refined and tested "in the furnace of affliction" (48:10)? How have such times affected the church?

3. a) Isaiah declares that when God called him to be a prophet, God made his "mouth like a sharp-edged sword" (49:2). From what you have read so far, in what ways does this description fit Isaiah's style of prophecy?

   b) How could this description of a way of speaking be applied to Jesus? (See Matt 10:34-36; Luke 2:34; 12:49-53; Rev 19:15.)

Lesson Three

4. Why do you suppose the image of being a "light to the nations" (49:6) had such power at the time of the Babylonian exile as well as for later generations? (See 49:8, 18, 23; Luke 2:25-32; Acts 1:8; 13:47.)

5. What experiences have you had or observed that might help to explain why God's people still felt forsaken and forgotten even when told they would be liberated (49:14)?

6. "I will never forget you. / See, upon the palms of my hands I have engraved you" (49:15-16). How might God's ancient promise to Israel assist you in your spiritual journey at this time in your life?

7. What does Isaiah tell God's people about the purpose of their exile (50:1)?

Lesson Three

8. The prophet Isaiah receives from God "a word that will waken" those who are weary (50:4). When have you seen God or God's word give new energy to those who have been made weary by life circumstances, injustices, or tragedies?

9. Select one of the accounts of the passion of Jesus from the Gospels and consider how the Servant Song of 50:4-11 corresponds with the suffering of Jesus. (See Matt 26:36–27:54; Mark 14:32–15:39; Luke 22:39–23:47; John 18:1–19:35.)

CLOSING PRAYER

Prayer

See, I refined you, but not like silver;
I tested you in the furnace of affliction.

(Isa 48:10)

We are always ready, Lord God, to accept good things from your hands. Help us also to accept the challenges and difficulties you allow. By your grace, may they bring us closer to you and to one another. Grant that we may embrace our crosses with humility and patience, especially . . .

LESSON FOUR

Isaiah 51–55

Begin your personal study and group discussion with a simple and sincere prayer such as:

Prayer

Lord God, as we continue our study of Isaiah, may our hearts remain open to the prophet's proclamation of your boundless love for your people. Inspire us with your Spirit so we may always be moved to seek you and to serve one another.

Read the Bible text of Isaiah 51–55 found in the outside columns of pages 60–68, highlighting what stands out to you.

Read the accompanying commentary to add to your understanding.

Respond to the questions on pages 69–71, Exploring Lesson Four.

The Closing Prayer on page 72 is for your personal use and may be used at the end of group discussion.

Lesson Four

CHAPTER 51

Exhortation To Trust in the Lord

¹Listen to me, you who pursue justice,
    who seek the LORD;
Look to the rock from which you were
    hewn,
    to the quarry from which you were taken;
²Look to Abraham, your father,
    and to Sarah, who gave you birth;
Though he was but one when I called him,
    I blessed him and made him many.
³Yes, the LORD shall comfort Zion,
    shall comfort all her ruins;
Her wilderness he shall make like Eden,
    her wasteland like the garden of the LORD;
Joy and gladness shall be found in her,
    thanksgiving and the sound of song.

⁴Be attentive to me, my people;
    my nation, give ear to me.
For teaching shall go forth from me,
    and my judgment, as light to the peoples.

continue

51:1-8 Salvation is coming

Here the prophet takes a more positive tack as he exhorts his fellow exiles to believe in the future of Jerusalem. He addresses his audience as "you who pursue justice," i.e., those actively committed to the establishment of a just society. He goes on to show that their dreams are realistic despite what appear to be great obstacles to their fulfillment.

Those who believe only a miracle could restore Judah ought to remember the story of Abraham and Sarah, their ancestors. God's promises to them were fulfilled although it appeared impossible for them ever to have children. God will effect another miracle to save the people of Jerusalem in exile. God will transform the city and its people in a way that is similar to the transformation of the desert into a beautiful garden.

Though the prophet uses the mythical image of Eden as a metaphor for the liberated Jerusalem, it is clear that he expects the transformation to take place through justice and the torah. Again recalling the words of 2:2-4, the prophet assures the exiles that all nations will recognize this triumph of justice. Though the heavens suggest permanency, they will be swept away before God's salvation and deliverance for Zion will fail. The people need to live by the torah and be unafraid of those who do not. The latter will be gone soon, but God's deliverance will be lasting. God's victory over the powers of chaos is another reason for the people's confidence. What God did once God can do again.

51:9–52:12 Awake!

The prophet's language is becoming more intense as he urges his fellow exiles to action. Three times in this passage he tells them to awake (51:9, 17; 52:1). The prophet again reminds the exiles of the power of God in creation. First, by using mythological imagery similar to that in 27:1, the prophet wants the exiles to see God as victorious in a primeval combat with the chaos monster Rahab (51:9-16). Confidence in God's power to liberate Jerusalem then is well founded. The exiles will return to Jerusalem. They should not fear what human beings can do to them because of what God promised to do for them. Their oppressors' power will end, and they will be released from captivity very soon. Using the same imagery as in 40:8, the prophet declares that God has assured Zion of its deliverance and the word of the Creator can be depended on.

The **repetition of commands** is a common stylistic device used in Second Isaiah. This device provides structure to the oracles in Isaiah 51, for example:

"Comfort, give comfort . . ."	40:1
"Awake, awake . . ."/ "Wake up, wake up . . ."	51:9, 17; 52:1
"Depart, depart . . ."	52:11

Second, Jerusalem, which has experienced divine judgment, should realize that judgment was not God's last word to it (51:17-23). Though Jerusalem experienced the loss of its children and military and natural disasters, there is a new day that is about to dawn. Zion will no longer have to drink the cup of judgment. That cup will pass to those nations that have been Zion's tormentors.

Finally, Zion has to rouse itself after the stupor caused by having to drink the cup of judgment (52:1-12). As it rises from the humiliation of captivity, the city will no longer be vulnerable to attack from outsiders. It will no longer be occupied by aliens nor tainted by the ritually impure. The bonds that have kept Zion captive are now falling away. The people whom God abandoned to slavery and captivity will experience the power of God's presence. The deliverance that Zion will experience will testify to the power and presence of God. Those returning from exile will bring good news to Jerusalem. From a distance, those who protect the city from surprise attack will see the procession of Jerusalem's exiles. They will be the first to hear the good news of the city's deliverance, so they will announce that deliverance by singing of

⁵I will make my victory come swiftly;
  my salvation shall go forth
  and my arm shall judge the nations;
In me the coastlands shall hope,
  and my arm they shall await.

⁶Raise your eyes to the heavens,
  look at the earth below;
Though the heavens vanish like smoke,
  the earth wear out like a garment
  and its inhabitants die like flies,
My salvation shall remain forever
  and my victory shall always be firm.
⁷Hear me, you who know justice,
  you people who have my teaching at heart:
Do not fear the reproach of others;
  remain firm at their revilings.
⁸They shall be like a garment eaten by moths,
  like wool consumed by grubs;
But my victory shall remain forever,
  my salvation, for all generations.

⁹Awake, awake, put on strength,
  arm of the LORD!
Awake as in the days of old,
  in ages long ago!
Was it not you who crushed Rahab,
  you who pierced the dragon?
¹⁰Was it not you who dried up the sea,
  the waters of the great deep,
You who made the depths of the sea into a way
  for the redeemed to pass through?
¹¹Those whom the LORD has ransomed will return
  and enter Zion singing,
  crowned with everlasting joy;
They will meet with joy and gladness,
  sorrow and mourning will flee.

¹²I, it is I who comfort you.
  Can you then fear mortals who die,
  human beings who are just grass,
¹³And forget the LORD, your maker,
  who stretched out the heavens
  and laid the foundations of earth?

continue

All the day you are in constant dread
   of the fury of the oppressor
When he prepares himself to destroy;
   but where is the oppressor's fury?

¹⁴The captives shall soon be released;
   they shall not die and go down into the pit,
   nor shall they want for bread.
¹⁵For I am the LORD, your God,
   who stirs up the sea so that its waves roar;
   the LORD of hosts by name.
¹⁶I have put my words into your mouth,
   I covered you, shielded by my hand,
Stretching out the heavens,
   laying the foundations of the earth,
   saying to Zion: You are my people.

The Cup of the Lord

¹⁷Wake up, wake up!
   Arise, Jerusalem,
You who drank at the LORD's hand
   the cup of his wrath;
Who drained to the dregs
   the bowl of staggering!
¹⁸She has no one to guide her
   of all the children she bore;
She has no one to take her by the hand,
   of all the children she reared!—
¹⁹Your misfortunes are double;
   who is there to grieve with you?
Desolation and destruction, famine and sword!
   Who is there to comfort you?
²⁰Your children lie helpless
   at every street corner
   like antelopes in a net.
They are filled with the wrath of the LORD,
   the rebuke of your God.

²¹But now, hear this, afflicted one,
   drunk, but not with wine,
²²Thus says the LORD, your Master,
   your God, who defends his people:
See, I am taking from your hand
   the cup of staggering;
The bowl of my wrath
   you shall no longer drink.
²³I will put it into the hands of your
         tormentors,
   those who said to you,
   "Bow down, that we may walk over you."
So you offered your back like the ground,
   like the street for them to walk on.

CHAPTER 52

Let Zion Rejoice

¹Awake, awake!
   Put on your strength, Zion;
Put on your glorious garments,
   Jerusalem, holy city.
Never again shall the uncircumcised
   or the unclean enter you.

continue

God's great victory over the powers that kept Zion in subjection. The people who return must make themselves ritually clean, because they will be entering the city made holy by God's presence.

The book of Revelation assumes that the prophet's vision of a new Jerusalem will be fulfilled only at the end of this age with the descent of the heavenly Jerusalem to earth (52:7; Rev 21:27). In Romans 10:15 Paul applies 52:7 to Christian preachers who bring the good news of Jesus to the Jews.

 An account of the return of the **vessels and utensils used in temple ritual** (52:11) is found in Ezra 1:7-11. These sacred items were removed by the forces of King Nebuchadnezzar when Jerusalem was sacked in 587 B.C. Ezra's inventory of looted items released by King Cyrus for restoration in the Jerusalem temple is extensive and includes over five thousand gold and silver vessels.

²Arise, shake off the dust,
    sit enthroned, Jerusalem;
Loose the bonds from your neck,
    captive daughter Zion!
³For thus says the LORD:
For nothing you were sold,
    without money you shall be redeemed.

⁴For thus says the Lord GOD:
To Egypt long ago my people went down,
    to sojourn there;
Assyria, too, oppressed them for nought.
⁵But now, what am I to do here?
    —oracle of the LORD.
My people have been taken away for
        nothing;
    their rulers mock, oracle of the LORD;
    constantly, every day, my name is reviled.
⁶Therefore my people shall know my name
    on that day, that it is I who speaks: Here
        I am!
⁷How beautiful upon the mountains
    are the feet of the one bringing good news,
Announcing peace, bearing good news,
    announcing salvation, saying to Zion,
        "Your God is King!"

⁸Listen! Your sentinels raise a cry,
    together they shout for joy,
For they see directly, before their eyes,
    the LORD's return to Zion.
⁹Break out together in song,
    O ruins of Jerusalem!
For the LORD has comforted his people,
    has redeemed Jerusalem.
¹⁰The LORD has bared his holy arm
    in the sight of all the nations;
All the ends of the earth can see
    the salvation of our God.

¹¹Depart, depart, go out from there,
    touch nothing unclean!
Out from there! Purify yourselves,
    you who carry the vessels of the LORD.
¹²But not in hurried flight will you go out,
    nor leave in headlong haste,
For the LORD goes before you,
    and your rear guard is the God of Israel.

Suffering and Triumph of the Servant of the Lord

¹³See, my servant shall prosper,
    he shall be raised high and greatly exalted.
¹⁴Even as many were amazed at him—
    so marred were his features,
    beyond that of mortals

continue

52:13–53:12 The Suffering Servant

After using feminine metaphors to describe the plight of Zion in some detail in chapters 51 and 52, the prophet returns to the masculine image of the Servant. Taking on the persona of God, the prophet proclaims the exaltation of the servant after his total humiliation. This will happen before the eyes of the kings responsible for the servant's suffering. Again the prophet announces the end of Judah's degradation.

In 53:1, the prophet speaks in the person of the kings who are witnessing the servant's exaltation. They cannot believe what they are seeing since they considered the servant of no account, someone who could be looked upon only with contempt. The kings then make an astonishing statement in verses 4-5. These verses appear to speak of vicarious atonement, i.e., that one person can bear the sin of another so as to remove the guilt of the second person. Such an idea is found nowhere else in the Old Testament. While this does not eliminate the possibility that the prophet was speaking about vicarious suffering, it should lead one to consider other possibilities. Perhaps what the prophet's rhetoric is expressing is an idea similar to that in Lamentations 5:7, i.e., that the preexilic generation actually committed the sin, but the exiles are the ones who have to bear the consequences.

his appearance, beyond that of human
  beings—
¹⁵So shall he startle many nations,
  kings shall stand speechless;
For those who have not been told shall see,
  those who have not heard shall ponder it.

CHAPTER 53

¹Who would believe what we have heard?
  To whom has the arm of the LORD been
    revealed?
²He grew up like a sapling before him,
  like a shoot from the parched earth;
He had no majestic bearing to catch our eye,
  no beauty to draw us to him.
³He was spurned and avoided by men,
  a man of suffering, knowing pain,
Like one from whom you turn your face,
  spurned, and we held him in no esteem.

⁴Yet it was our pain that he bore,
  our sufferings he endured.
We thought of him as stricken,
  struck down by God and afflicted,
⁵But he was pierced for our sins,
  crushed for our iniquity.
He bore the punishment that makes us
    whole,
  by his wounds we were healed.
⁶We had all gone astray like sheep,
  all following our own way;
But the LORD laid upon him
  the guilt of us all.

⁷Though harshly treated, he submitted
  and did not open his mouth;
Like a lamb led to slaughter
  or a sheep silent before shearers,
  he did not open his mouth.
⁸Seized and condemned, he was taken away.
  Who would have thought any more of his
    destiny?
For he was cut off from the land of the living,
  struck for the sins of his people.

continue

Another way to understand 53:4-5 is to see these verses as the prophet's attempt to broaden his contemporaries' understanding of their suffering beyond punishment for sin. While the prophet did affirm more than once that Jerusalem's suffering was God's judgment on its infidelity (42:18-22, 24-25; 43:24; 47:6), he also maintained that the city's punishment was out of proportion to its guilt (40:2). What then was the point of the exile? Jerusalem's suffering was part of God's work in the world. The nations will see what God has done and will do for Zion and be led to join Judah in the worship of its God. The people's suffering and exaltation then enable them to be God's witnesses (43:9-10) as they fulfill their mission to be "a light for the nations" (42:6; 49:6).

The poem concludes with God speaking in the first person just as the poem began (52:13-14; 53:11-13). God describes the vindication of the servant. In fact, the poem as a whole is a dramatization of the servant's final triumph. This is reminiscent of a thanksgiving psalm, but with certain modifications. In thanksgiving psalms, the person who has been rescued speaks. Here the servant is silent. God describes the servant's vindication. Second, people listen to the testimony of the one rescued in a thanksgiving psalm, but here the people themselves testify to the marvels that they have witnessed.

Of all Isaianic texts, this one has resonated most with the Christian belief in Jesus and in the significance of his suffering and death. There are about forty citations or allusions to this text in the New Testament. This testifies to the power of the prophetic word. Matthew also cites this text in commenting on Jesus' healing of Peter's mother-in-law (Matt 8:17).

The problem of suffering is one of those issues that confronts believers in every religious tradition. It was a special problem for the first Christians, who had to make sense of the tragic death of Jesus. They found this passage especially meaningful. The prophet was able to help the exiles see that their suffering was more than a judgment upon the sins of their elders. It was the means by which Judah could

⁹He was given a grave among the wicked,
  a burial place with evildoers,
Though he had done no wrong,
  nor was deceit found in his mouth.
¹⁰But it was the LORD's will to crush him
    with pain.
By making his life as a reparation offering,
  he shall see his offspring, shall lengthen
    his days,
  and the LORD's will shall be accomplished
    through him.
¹¹Because of his anguish he shall see the light;
  because of his knowledge he shall be
    content;
My servant, the just one, shall justify the many,
  their iniquity he shall bear.
¹²Therefore I will give him his portion
    among the many,
  and he shall divide the spoils with the
    mighty,
Because he surrendered himself to death,
  was counted among the transgressors,
Bore the sins of many,
  and interceded for the transgressors.

CHAPTER 54

The New Zion

¹Raise a glad cry, you barren one who never bore a child,
  break forth in jubilant song, you who
    have never been in labor,
For more numerous are the children of the
    deserted wife
  than the children of her who has a husband,
    says the LORD.
²Enlarge the space for your tent,
  spread out your tent cloths unsparingly;
  lengthen your ropes and make firm your
    pegs.
³For you shall spread abroad to the right and
    left;
  your descendants shall dispossess the
    nations
  and shall people the deserted cities.

⁴Do not fear, you shall not be put to shame;
  do not be discouraged, you shall not be
    disgraced.

continue

fulfill its mission as a light to the nations. The prophet has articulated one of the great paradoxes of the biblical tradition: victory comes through defeat, exaltation through humiliation, life from death. This is how the first Christians came to understand the cross.

The idea of a *substitutive sacrifice* was an integral part of Israelite ritual. Isaiah 53:10 is a clear reference to this type of sacrifice, as the death of the servant is called a **"reparation offering"** (*reparation* has the sense of "repaying" or "making right"; see Lev 5:14-26; 7:1-6; 14:21-28). Perhaps the best known of such sacrifices is that which occurred annually on the Day of Atonement (Lev 16:1-22).

54:1-17 Zion is reconciled with God

The focus of this passage is on reconciliation and its effects. A husband promises never again to lose his temper, never again to walk out on his wife, never again to leave her childless and humiliated. Though the cause of the rift was partly the woman's fault, the husband takes primary responsibility for the tragedy and swears that he will never again be angry with her. The reconciliation makes possible "enduring love" and a "covenant of peace" that is more lasting than the hills (54:8, 10). But first he must convince her that he really loves her and that she can trust him. The image of God painted by the prophet here is that of a husband who gives in to a temporary fit of anger but whose love of his wife is forever. Of course, Zion represents the exiles as verse 17 makes clear. Also, the verb in verse 7, trans-

For the shame of your youth you shall forget,
  the reproach of your widowhood no
    longer remember.
⁵For your husband is your Maker;
  the LORD of hosts is his name,
Your redeemer, the Holy One of Israel,
  called God of all the earth.

⁶The LORD calls you back,
  like a wife forsaken and grieved in spirit,
A wife married in youth and then cast off,
  says your God.
⁷For a brief moment I abandoned you,
  but with great tenderness I will take you
    back.
⁸In an outburst of wrath, for a moment
  I hid my face from you;
But with enduring love I take pity on you,
  says the LORD, your redeemer.

⁹This is for me like the days of Noah:
As I swore then that the waters of Noah
  should never again flood the earth,
So I have sworn now not to be angry with you,
  or to rebuke you.
¹⁰Though the mountains fall away
  and the hills be shaken,
My love shall never fall away from you
  nor my covenant of peace be shaken,
  says the LORD, who has mercy on you.

¹¹O afflicted one, storm-battered and
    unconsoled,
  I lay your pavements in carnelians,
  your foundations in sapphires;
¹²I will make your battlements of rubies,
  your gates of jewels,
  and all your walls of precious stones.
¹³All your children shall be taught by the
    LORD;
  great shall be the peace of your children.
¹⁴In justice shall you be established,
  far from oppression, you shall not fear,
  from destruction, it cannot come near.
¹⁵If there be an attack, it is not my doing;
  whoever attacks shall fall before you.

continue

lated as "I will take you back," is a technical term for the ingathering of the exiles and points to a collective interpretation of the woman.

Following the lead of the Septuagint, Paul applies verse 1 to Sarah (see Gen 15), who becomes the mother of Isaac and ultimately to all the children of the promise as he applies this text to the church, the new Jerusalem (Gal 4:27-28).

55:1-13 The return to Zion

The prophet urges the exiles to return to Jerusalem. His appeal begins with an offer of food and drink to the hungry and thirsty. This food and drink bring life, the source of which is the covenant made between God and those invited to the feast. While the prophet speaks of the "everlasting covenant" made with David, he does not envision the restoration of the Davidic dynasty. He transforms the Davidic covenant by asserting that the role once played by Judah's kings in the past will be fulfilled by a much wider circle in the future. The second person plural "you" in verse 3 makes it clear that the exiles, who are returning to Jerusalem, will be the witnesses to God's power. Those who accept God's invitation to the banquet (the experience of God's presence in Jerusalem) have life through the covenant, which makes God's glory shine through them.

Through the prophet, God summons the exiles to God's sanctuary in Jerusalem. But to enter the sanctuary is to enter into God's presence. Those who come into God's presence must reject patterns of inappropriate behavior (see Pss 15; 25; Isa 33:14-16). While Jerusalem is not mentioned specifically, the clear implication of this text is that an authentic encounter with God can take place only in Zion (see Jer 29:10-14). The time of exile was a special circumstance, but once Babylon has fallen, Jerusalem can be restored to its unique status in Israel. Just as all physical life on earth is dependent upon the moisture that comes from the sky, so Jerusalem's restoration is dependent upon God. But God has spoken. Zion's future is assured.

¹⁶See, I have created the smith
   who blows on the burning coals
   and forges weapons as his work;
It is I also who have created
   the destroyer to work havoc.
¹⁷Every weapon fashioned against you shall fail;
   every tongue that brings you to trial
   you shall prove false.

This is the lot of the servants of the Lord,
   their vindication from me—oracle of the Lord.

CHAPTER 55

An Invitation to Grace

¹All you who are thirsty,
   come to the water!
You who have no money,
   come, buy grain and eat;
Come, buy grain without money,
   wine and milk without cost!
²Why spend your money for what is not bread;
   your wages for what does not satisfy?
Only listen to me, and you shall eat well,
   you shall delight in rich fare.
³Pay attention and come to me;
   listen, that you may have life.
I will make with you an everlasting covenant,
   the steadfast loyalty promised to David.
⁴As I made him a witness to peoples,
   a leader and commander of peoples,
⁵So shall you summon a nation you knew not,
   and a nation that knew you not shall run to you,
Because of the Lord, your God,
   the Holy One of Israel, who has glorified you.

⁶Seek the Lord while he may be found,
   call upon him while he is near.
⁷Let the wicked forsake their way,
   and sinners their thoughts;
Let them turn to the Lord to find mercy;
   to our God, who is generous in forgiving.
⁸For my thoughts are not your thoughts,
   nor are your ways my ways—oracle of the Lord.
⁹For as the heavens are higher than the earth,
   so are my ways higher than your ways,
   my thoughts higher than your thoughts.

¹⁰Yet just as from the heavens
   the rain and snow come down
And do not return there
   till they have watered the earth,
   making it fertile and fruitful,
Giving seed to the one who sows
   and bread to the one who eats,
¹¹So shall my word be
   that goes forth from my mouth;
It shall not return to me empty,
   but shall do what pleases me,
   achieving the end for which I sent it.

continue

The prophet calls the exiles to take the first steps back to Jerusalem where the Lord can be found. The desert that stands between Babylon and Judah has been stripped of its power to interfere with the glorious procession that will bring the exiles back to Zion. This is a reprise of the opening vision of the prophecy (40:3-5). The image that the prophet is creating is one which sees God at the head of a great throng of Israelites who are making their way back to their homeland after years of exile. Nature is transformed miraculously to ease their journey. They are returning to Zion where they can seek and find God (see Isa 33:20-22).

Paul quotes verse 10 as he tries to motivate the Corinthians to contribute to the collection that he is making for the poor of Jerusalem (2 Cor 9:10-11).

Lesson Four

> ¹²Yes, in joy you shall go forth,
>   in peace you shall be brought home;
> Mountains and hills shall break out in song
>   before you,
>   all trees of the field shall clap their hands.
> ¹³In place of the thornbush, the cypress shall
>   grow,
>   instead of nettles, the myrtle.
> This shall be to the LORD's renown,
>   as an everlasting sign that shall not fail.

 The **call for social justice** throughout Isaiah continues to be a focus of church teaching today. *Pacem in Terris*, an encyclical by Pope Saint John XXIII, grounds the rights of all persons in their shared human nature and common creation by God. The Second Vatican Council clearly denounced as opposed to the teaching of Christ any policy that discriminates against people based on their race, color, economic status, or religion. Our belief in the Trinity is a reminder that God's very nature is relational. God's relational nature is extended to human persons in creation and in covenant. Consequently, inclusion is a central dimension of faith communities.

Lesson Four

EXPLORING LESSON FOUR

1. What is the prophet's purpose in recalling Abraham and Sarah (51:1-3) and the flight from Egypt (51:10-11)? (See Gen 12:1-3; 22:17-18; Exod 14:19-31.)

2. What is the significance of the prophet's repeated references to justice throughout 51:1-8? (See 1:27; 2:2-4; Deut 16:20; 32:4; Ezra 9:15; Ps 37:27-28; 146:5-8.)

3. a) What factors contributed to Israel's need to be awakened (51:17; 52:1)?

   b) What factors today contribute to our spiritual drowsiness?

4. a) How does Paul use Isaiah 52:7 in Romans 10:14-17?

Lesson Four

b) Who has been an ambassador of the "good news" in your life (52:7)?

5. According to the commentary, what are some possible meanings of the servant bearing the pain and suffering of others and being "pierced" for their sins (53:4-6)?

6. In what ways has the church helped to draw out additional understandings of the suffering described throughout this Servant Song (52:13–53:12)? (See Matt 8:16-17; 9:35-36; John 10:11-18; Acts 8:26-35; 1 Pet 2:21-25.)

7. How does the message of redemptive suffering found in the Servant Songs (42:1-4; 49:1-6; 50:4-9; 52:13–53:12) affected your attitude toward personal suffering?

Lesson Four

8. How does barrenness and its reversal serve as an appropriate metaphor for the spiritual condition of God's people (54:1-3)? (See Gen 18:9-14; 30:22-23; 1 Sam 1:4-11; Ps 113:7-9.)

9. What qualities of the marriage relationship alluded to in 54:4-10 are also the qualities of God's relationship to us?

10. By using imperatives ("[p]ay attention," "come to me," "listen," and "[s]eek the Lord"; 55:3, 6), Isaiah makes it clear that the returning exiles must actively participate in their liberation. Where or when might God be using these same imperatives today?

CLOSING PRAYER

Prayer

*Though the mountains fall away
 and the hills be shaken,
My love shall never fall away from you
 nor my covenant of peace be shaken,
 says the L*ORD*, who has mercy on you.*

(Isa 54:10)

How wonderful is your love, Lord our God! Even when we fail to walk in your ways, you remain a flowing river of mercy and compassion. We raise our voices in thanksgiving and promise to express our gratitude in action by sharing your love with others, especially . . .

LESSON FIVE

Isaiah 56–61

Begin your personal study and group discussion with a simple and sincere prayer such as:

Prayer

Lord God, as we continue our study of Isaiah, may our hearts remain open to the prophet's proclamation of your boundless love for your people. Inspire us with your Spirit so we may always be moved to seek you and to serve one another.

Read the Bible text of Isaiah 56–61 found in the outside columns of pages 74–85, highlighting what stands out to you.

Read the accompanying commentary to add to your understanding.

Respond to the questions on pages 86–88, Exploring Lesson Five.

The Closing Prayer on page 89 is for your personal use and may be used at the end of group discussion.

III. Isaiah 56–66

CHAPTER 56

Salvation for the Just

¹Thus says the LORD:
Observe what is right, do what is just,
  for my salvation is about to come,
  my justice, about to be revealed.
²Happy is the one who does this,
  whoever holds fast to it:
Keeping the sabbath without profaning it,
  keeping one's hand from doing any evil.

Obligations and Promises to Share in the Covenant

³The foreigner joined to the LORD should
    not say,
  "The LORD will surely exclude me from
    his people";
Nor should the eunuch say,
  "See, I am a dry tree."
⁴For thus says the LORD:
To the eunuchs who keep my sabbaths,
  who choose what pleases me,
  and who hold fast to my covenant,
⁵I will give them, in my house
  and within my walls, a monument and a
    name
Better than sons and daughters;
  an eternal name, which shall not be cut
    off, will I give them.
⁶And foreigners who join themselves to the
    LORD,
  to minister to him,
To love the name of the LORD,
  to become his servants—
All who keep the sabbath without profaning it
  and hold fast to my covenant,
⁷Them I will bring to my holy mountain
  and make them joyful in my house of
    prayer;
Their burnt offerings and their sacrifices
  will be acceptable on my altar,

continue

THE NEW JERUSALEM

Isaiah 56:1–66:24

The image of the Creator who subdued the powers of chaos, leading the exiles back to Jerusalem and initiating a glorious restoration that will amaze the nations, gives way to a more realistic picture in the final section of the book of Isaiah. Some exiles have returned to Jerusalem, but the restoration is sputtering. The prophet observes that the old social trappings are reemerging, that the people are not committed to their identity as Jews, and that their religious observance is inauthentic because it is not founded on a commitment to justice. Despite this, the prophet is still able to speak about the future of Jerusalem in a lyrical and expansive mode. He envisions a new Jerusalem repopulated with those who pursue righteousness and joined in the worship of Yahweh by all nations.

56:1-8 The sabbath

The prophet uses a strategy that presents sabbath observance as an element of Jewish identity and then goes on to expand the parameters of that identity. The observance of the sabbath came to have great significance in the Jewish community as an identity-marker. The preexilic markers of Judahite identity such as the national state and native dynasty were gone. Traditional practices such as sabbath observance, circumcision, and the dietary laws began to take on new significance. This passage mentions the need to keep the sabbath three times (56:2, 4, 6). It also broadens the scope of the people of God. The community, of course, includes the descendants of Abraham (see 48:1; 51:2; 63:16), but also those people who can claim no such descent but who, nonetheless, observe the sabbath and keep the covenant. God will bring these people to Jerusalem and to the temple, which is here called a "house of prayer for all peoples" (56:7; see 1 Kgs 8:41-43). God will not only bring the exiles back to Jerusalem but will call the nations to become part of God's people. What is important for inclusion among this people, then, is not physical descent from a common ancestor but careful observance of God's will.

Verses 3b-5 mention eunuchs, i.e., castrated males. In the monarchic period, eunuchs were members of the royal court (see 1 Sam 8:15; 1 Kgs 22:9; 2 Kgs 8:6). This passage focuses not on their social position but on their physical condition. Deuteronomic law excluded eunuchs from Judah's religious assemblies (Deut 23:1). The prophet did not. Also, eunuchs, who were afraid that they would be forgotten without descendants to remember them, are promised "a monument and a name" in the new Jerusalem. The Hebrew phrase *yad vashem* ("a monument and a name") is the title given to Jerusalem's memorial to the Holocaust. The title is inspired by verse 5 and the memorial is so named because entire families were exterminated in the Holocaust, leaving no one to remember them.

In the story of Jesus' cleansing of the temple, the Synoptic Gospels have Jesus cite verse 7 as a justification for his action, though only Mark cites that part of the prophet's words which call the temple a place of prayer "for all peoples" (Matt 21:13; Mark 11:17; Luke 19:46). But the allusion to the Isaianic text sees the universalism of the messianic age fulfilled through the proclamation of the gospel.

> For my house shall be called
>   a house of prayer for all peoples.
> ⁸Oracle of the Lord GOD,
>   who gathers the dispersed of Israel—
> Others will I gather to them
>   besides those already gathered.
>
> **Unworthy Shepherds**
>
> ⁹All you beasts of the field,
>   come to devour,
>   all you beasts in the forest!
> ¹⁰All the sentinels of Israel are blind,
>   they are without knowledge;
> They are all mute dogs,
>   unable to bark;
> Dreaming, reclining,
>   loving their sleep.
> ¹¹Yes, the dogs have a ravenous appetite;
>   they never know satiety,
> Shepherds who have no understanding;
>   all have turned their own way,
>   each one covetous for gain:
> ¹²"Come, let me bring wine;
>   let us fill ourselves with strong drink,
> And tomorrow will be like today,
>   or even greater."
>
> *continue*

56:9-12 Corrupt leaders

The restored Jerusalem community was not blessed with good leadership. Too often its "sentinels" used their position to enrich themselves at the expense of those over whom they were to watch. What was worse was that their appetite had no limits. The prophet refers to them as "dogs" (56:11). This was a particularly insulting affront. Dogs were not kept as pets but were scavengers living on the outskirts of cities and towns, living off refuse and carrion. The prophet also accuses the community's leaders for toasting to their good fortune and their plans for more profits at the expense of the poor.

CHAPTER 57

¹The just have perished,
  but no one takes it to heart;
The steadfast are swept away,
  while no one understands.
Yet the just are taken away from the presence
    of evil,
  ²and enter into peace;
They rest upon their couches,
  the sincere, who walk in integrity.

An Idolatrous People

³But you, draw near,
  you children of a sorceress,
    offspring of an adulterer and a prostitute!
⁴Against whom do you make sport,
  against whom do you open wide your
      mouth,
    and stick out your tongue?
Are you not rebellious children,
  deceitful offspring—
⁵You who burn with lust among the oaks,
  under every green tree;
You who immolate children in the wadies,
  among the clefts of the rocks?
⁶Among the smooth stones of the wadi is
      your portion,
  they, they are your allotment;
Indeed, you poured out a drink offering to
      them,
  and brought up grain offerings.
  With these things, should I be appeased?
⁷Upon a towering and lofty mountain
  you set up your bed,
    and there you went up to offer sacrifice.
⁸Behind the door and the doorpost
  you set up your symbol.
Yes, deserting me, you carried up your
      bedding;
    and spread it wide.
You entered an agreement with them,
  you loved their couch, you gazed upon
      nakedness.

continue

57:1-13 Against idolatry

The prophet associates an unjust social system with the worship of other gods. He continues his criticism of a corrupt leadership class by noting that these leaders do not pay any attention to the death of just people. Their passing goes unnoticed by those whose attention is centered on their own aggrandizement. The prophet has no use for Jerusalem's religious leadership and accuses them of idolatry and associated practices including child sacrifice. The intensity of the language here makes it clear that there was a serious division in the Jewish community. Clearly the prophet aligns himself not with the leaders but with those who are oppressed by an incompetent and unjust upper class. The prophet concludes his diatribe by ridiculing idolatry. He claims that gods other than the Lord are powerless to help their worshipers. Only those who remain faithful to Israel's ancestral deity will be secure. Serving other gods is a prelude to destruction.

The prophet's words likely reflect a genuine social and religious conflict between those elements of early Jewish society who wished to remain true to their ancestral religious traditions and those who were ready to accommodate themselves to the political, social, and economic realities of the day. Their accommodation expresses itself in their willingness to abandon their own religious traditions in favor of those of their occupiers.

 The practice of **child sacrifice** (57:5), though explicitly prohibited by the torah (Deut 18:10; Lev 18:21), was sporadically practiced in Judah from the eighth century B.C., reflecting the practices of neighboring peoples. Sacrifices were conducted in the Hinnom Valley, just outside the walls of Jerusalem (see map on p. 12). Jesus makes use of the evil history of this place, well-known to his contemporaries, when he refers to Gehenna (Hebrew *ge-hinnōm*, "valley of the son of Hinnom") as an image of fiery divine punishment (Matt 18:9; Mark 9:43; Luke 12:5).

⁹You approached the king with oil,
  and multiplied your perfumes;
You sent your ambassadors far away,
  down even to deepest Sheol.
¹⁰Though worn out with the length of your
    journey,
  you never said, "It is hopeless";
You found your strength revived,
  and so you did not weaken.
¹¹Whom did you dread and fear,
  that you told lies,
And me you did not remember
  nor take to heart?
Am I to keep silent and conceal,
  while you show no fear of me?
¹²I will proclaim your justice
  and your works;
  but they shall not help you.
¹³When you cry out,
  let your collection of idols save you.
All these the wind shall carry off,
  a mere breath shall bear them away;
But whoever takes refuge in me shall inherit
    the land,
  and possess my holy mountain.

The Way to Peace for God's People

¹⁴And I say:
Build up, build up, prepare the way,
  remove every obstacle from my people's
    way.

¹⁵For thus says the high and lofty One,
  the One who dwells forever, whose name
    is holy:
I dwell in a high and holy place,
  but also with the contrite and lowly of
    spirit,
To revive the spirit of the lowly,
  to revive the heart of the crushed.
¹⁶For I will not accuse forever,
  nor always be angry;
For without me their spirit fails,
  the life breath that I have given.
¹⁷Because of their wicked avarice I grew
    angry;
  I struck them, hiding myself from them in
    wrath.
But they turned back, following the way
  of their own heart.
¹⁸I saw their ways,
  but I will heal them.
I will lead them and restore full comfort to
    them
  and to those who mourn for them,
¹⁹creating words of comfort.
Peace! Peace to those who are far and near,
  says the Lord; and I will heal them.
²⁰But the wicked are like the tossing sea
  which cannot be still,
Its waters cast up mire and mud.
²¹There is no peace for the wicked! says
  my God.

continue

57:14-21 The two ways

Although the corrupt leadership of Judah had control of the religious symbols of Judaism (e.g., the temple of Jerusalem), the prophet assures people that God dwells with the humble and contrite. The prophet, speaking in the name of God, asserts that the road of repentance is always open to those who have abandoned their religious traditions. Still, the wicked who refuse to repent cannot expect peace from God. The contrast between the "lowly" and the wicked is reminiscent of other descriptions of the "two ways," such as Psalm 1 and Jeremiah 17:5-8. The community in Jerusalem was experiencing a recurrence of the divisions that the prophet believes led to the fall of the city and the end of its political and religious institutions. He reaffirms his belief that God is with the poor and will judge their oppressors.

Lesson Five

CHAPTER 58

Reasons for Judgment

¹Cry out full-throated and unsparingly,
   lift up your voice like a trumpet blast;
Proclaim to my people their transgression,
   to the house of Jacob their sins.
²They seek me day after day,
   and desire to know my ways,
Like a nation that has done what is just
   and not abandoned the judgment of their
      God;
They ask of me just judgments,
   they desire to draw near to God.
³"Why do we fast, but you do not see it?
   afflict ourselves, but you take no note?"
See, on your fast day you carry out your own
      pursuits,
   and drive all your laborers.
⁴See, you fast only to quarrel and fight
   and to strike with a wicked fist!
Do not fast as you do today
   to make your voice heard on high!
⁵Is this the manner of fasting I would choose,
   a day to afflict oneself?
To bow one's head like a reed,
   and lie upon sackcloth and ashes?
Is this what you call a fast,
   a day acceptable to the LORD?

Authentic Fasting That Leads to Blessing

⁶Is this not, rather, the fast that I choose:
   releasing those bound unjustly,
   untying the thongs of the yoke;
Setting free the oppressed,
   breaking off every yoke?
⁷Is it not sharing your bread with the hungry,
   bringing the afflicted and the homeless
      into your house;
Clothing the naked when you see them,
   and not turning your back on your own
      flesh?
⁸Then your light shall break forth like the
      dawn,

continue

58:1-12 Fasting

Jerusalem's restoration was not proceeding according to expectations. The people had been fasting to elicit God's mercy, but to no avail. In early Judaism, fasting was not an ascetical practice. It was associated with mourning. The purpose of the fasts that came into vogue during the restoration (see Zech 8:18) was to move God to pity Jerusalem and hasten the day of its complete renewal. What the prophet decries here is not the practice of fasting but the ignorance of those who engaged in this practice. After all that the people of Judah have been through, they still have not learned that God expects them to create and maintain a society of justice and equity for all. The performance of ritual actions, no matter how well intentioned, is not a substitute for such a society. As long as injustice, oppression, and internal conflicts plague Judah, the restoration will be stalled. God wants Judah to "fast" from injustice. God wants the people of means to share their food, clothing, and shelter with their brothers and sisters who lack them. When Judah becomes a society based on compassion rather than oppression, justice rather than injustice, the restoration will go forward. Until then, Judah can expect nothing but divine judgment on an unjust and uncaring society. God will honor a just society with the divine presence.

 The **fasting** described in 58:3-7 is a fast from injustice, oppression, and social oppression. The entire society is invited to change social patterns so that justice, freedom, and provision of basic human needs are the norm for daily life. Catholic social teaching stresses that all persons should have access to whatever is necessary for leading a fully human life.

58:13-14 The sabbath

The observance of the sabbath became a significant form of Jewish self-identity following the return from Babylon. The national state and dynasty were not going to be restored. Despite

and your wound shall quickly be healed;
Your vindication shall go before you,
and the glory of the LORD shall be your rear guard.
⁹Then you shall call, and the LORD will answer,
you shall cry for help, and he will say: "Here I am!"
If you remove the yoke from among you,
the accusing finger, and malicious speech;
¹⁰If you lavish your food on the hungry
and satisfy the afflicted;
Then your light shall rise in the darkness,
and your gloom shall become like midday;
¹¹Then the LORD will guide you always
and satisfy your thirst in parched places,
will give strength to your bones
And you shall be like a watered garden,
like a flowing spring whose waters never fail.
¹²Your people shall rebuild the ancient ruins;
the foundations from ages past you shall raise up;
"Repairer of the breach," they shall call you,
"Restorer of ruined dwellings."

Authentic Sabbath Observance That Leads to Blessing

¹³If you refrain from trampling the sabbath,
from following your own pursuits on my holy day;
If you call the sabbath a delight,
the LORD's holy day glorious;
If you glorify it by not following your ways,
seeking your own interests, or pursuing your own affairs—
¹⁴Then you shall delight in the LORD,
and I will make you ride upon the heights of the earth;
I will nourish you with the heritage of Jacob, your father,
for the mouth of the LORD has spoken.

CHAPTER 59

Salvation Delayed

¹No, the hand of the LORD is not too short to save,
nor his ear too dull to hear.
²Rather, it is your crimes
that separate you from your God,
It is your sins that make him hide his face
so that he does not hear you.
³For your hands are defiled with blood,
and your fingers with crime;
Your lips speak falsehood,
and your tongue utters deceit.
⁴No one brings suit justly,
no one pleads truthfully;
They trust an empty plea and tell lies;
they conceive mischief and bring forth malice.
⁵They hatch adders' eggs,
and weave spiders' webs:

continue

encouragement and support from the Persians, more than twenty years elapsed before the temple was rebuilt. The sabbath then came to have new meaning. It was not simply a day of rest; it became a symbol of commitment to Judah's ancestral religion. The prophet suggests that if the people of Judah neglect the sabbath, they are rejecting their identity as the people of God. Observance of the sabbath, then, is an essential component of Jerusalem's restoration.

59:1-21 God will establish justice

Though God has ended the power of Judah's enemies and brought back its people from exile, the restoration was a profound disappointment. What was disappointing was not the lack of God's action but the people's response to it. Instead of creating a new society, the people were at war with each other. The old social and economic divisions that tore apart Israelite society in the monarchic period

Whoever eats the eggs will die,
  if one of them is crushed, it will hatch a
    viper;
⁶Their webs cannot serve as clothing,
  nor can they cover themselves with their
    works.
Their works are evil works,
  and deeds of violence are in their hands.
⁷Their feet run to evil,
  and they hasten to shed innocent blood;
Their thoughts are thoughts of wickedness,
  violence and destruction are on their
    highways.
⁸The way of peace they know not,
  and there is no justice on their paths;
Their roads they have made crooked,
  no one who walks in them knows peace.

Acknowledgment of Transgressions

⁹That is why judgment is far from us
  and justice does not reach us.
We look for light, but there is darkness;
  for brightness, and we walk in gloom!

¹⁰Like those who are blind we grope along
    the wall,
  like people without eyes we feel our way.
We stumble at midday as if at twilight,
  among the vigorous, we are like the dead.
¹¹Like bears we all growl,
  like doves we moan without ceasing.
We cry out for justice, but it is not there;
  for salvation, but it is far from us.
¹²For our transgressions before you are
    many,
  our sins bear witness against us.
Our transgressions are present to us,
  and our crimes we acknowledge:
¹³Transgressing, and denying the LORD,
  turning back from following our God,
Planning fraud and treachery,
  uttering lying words conceived in the
    heart.
¹⁴Judgment is turned away,
  and justice stands far off;
For truth stumbles in the public square,
  and uprightness cannot enter.

continue

were beginning to reassert themselves. This social conflict had the power to destroy Judah again as it had before.

The first step in reversing this process is the community's confession of sin. People have to take responsibility for creating a society that is self-destructive. The sad state of Judahite society is testimony to the failure of its people to incarnate the prophet's vision, a vision of a society of justice and truth. The people's failures cause God to act since God cannot ignore what the people are doing to themselves. God's judgment will come again on Jerusalem since God always acts for the sake of the oppressed. The prophet affirms that God's intention to restore Judah will not be frustrated by the people's actions. Since God has chosen Zion, God will restore Zion in spite of the failures of some of the people.

In speaking about the universal dominion of sin, Paul strings together several citations from the Old Testament, among them verses 7-8 (Rom 3:15-17). He also uses the images of "justice as his breastplate" and "victory as a helmet" (59:17) in Ephesians 6:14-17 and 1 Thessalonians 5:8.

 Two poems in Third Isaiah (59:15-21; 63:1-6) describe **God as a divine warrior**, wreaking vengeance on enemies and delivering God's people. The tradition of God as a warrior begins with the exodus: "The LORD will fight for you; you only have to keep still" (Exod 14:14; cf. 15:3-10). This concept does not legitimize violence or war; note that in this tradition, God fights alone (see Isa 59:16; 63:5).

¹⁵Fidelity is lacking,
    and whoever turns from evil is despoiled.

Divine Intervention

The LORD saw this, and was aggrieved
    that there was no justice.
¹⁶He saw that there was no one,
    was appalled that there was none to intervene;
Then his own arm brought about the victory,
    and his justice sustained him.
¹⁷He put on justice as his breastplate,
    victory as a helmet on his head;
He clothed himself with garments of vengeance,
    wrapped himself in a mantle of zeal.
¹⁸According to their deeds he repays his enemies
    and requites his foes with wrath;
to the coastlands he renders recompense.
¹⁹Those in the west shall fear the name of the LORD,
    and those in the east, his glory,
Coming like a pent-up stream
    driven on by the breath of the LORD.
²⁰Then for Zion shall come a redeemer,
    to those in Jacob who turn from transgression—oracle of the LORD.
²¹This is my covenant with them,
    which I myself have made, says the LORD:
My spirit which is upon you
    and my words that I have put in your mouth
Shall not depart from your mouth,
    nor from the mouths of your children
Nor the mouths of your children's children
    from this time forth and forever, says the LORD.

CHAPTER 60

The Dawning of Divine Glory for Zion

¹Arise! Shine, for your light has come,
    the glory of the LORD has dawned upon you.
²Though darkness covers the earth,
    and thick clouds, the peoples,
Upon you the LORD will dawn,
    and over you his glory will be seen.
³Nations shall walk by your light,
    kings by the radiance of your dawning.

The Nations Come to Zion

⁴Raise your eyes and look about;
    they all gather and come to you—
Your sons from afar,
    your daughters in the arms of their nurses.
⁵Then you shall see and be radiant,
    your heart shall throb and overflow.

continue

60:1-22 The glory of the new Jerusalem

The prophet shifts abruptly from a description of Jerusalem's halting restoration to a utopian picture of the new Jerusalem. Zion here is personified as a woman basking in the glow of God's light. The city, which has been a vassal of more powerful states for more than three hundred years, will be the place from which Yahweh rules the world. In fact, the rulers of those states that held Jerusalem in subjection will serve as workmen in rebuilding the city's walls. The nations will contribute to the outfitting of the new temple. Prosperity and security will be the marks of the "City of the LORD" and "Zion of the Holy One of Israel." As is clear from chapters 58–59, the prophet's vision has yet to be transformed into reality. Still, he is certain that God will bring all this about "swiftly" (60:22).

Two aspects of the prophet's vision call for comment. First is what has been described as "universalism." The nations are welcomed in Jerusalem. In fact, those nations that do not see the hand of the Lord in Zion's restoration will

For the riches of the sea shall be poured out
    before you,
  the wealth of nations shall come to you.
⁶Caravans of camels shall cover you,
  dromedaries of Midian and Ephah;
All from Sheba shall come
  bearing gold and frankincense,
  and heralding the praises of the LORD.
⁷All the flocks of Kedar shall be gathered for
    you,
  the rams of Nebaioth shall serve your
    needs;
They will be acceptable offerings on my altar,
  and I will glorify my glorious house.
⁸Who are these that fly along like a cloud,
  like doves to their cotes?
⁹The vessels of the coastlands are gathering,
  with the ships of Tarshish in the lead,
To bring your children from afar,
  their silver and gold with them—
For the name of the LORD, your God,
  for the Holy One of Israel who has
    glorified you.

Honor and Service for Zion

¹⁰Foreigners shall rebuild your walls,
  their kings shall minister to you;
Though in my wrath I struck you,
  yet in my good will I have shown you
    mercy.
¹¹Your gates shall stand open constantly;
  day and night they shall not be closed
So that they may bring you the wealth of
    nations,
  with their kings in the vanguard.
¹²For the nation or kingdom that will not
    serve you shall perish;
  such nations shall be utterly destroyed!
¹³The glory of Lebanon shall come to you—
  the juniper, the fir, and the cypress all
    together—
To bring beauty to my sanctuary,
  and glory to the place where I stand.

¹⁴The children of your oppressors shall come,
  bowing before you;
All those who despised you,
  shall bow low at your feet.
They shall call you "City of the LORD,"
  "Zion of the Holy One of Israel."
¹⁵No longer forsaken and hated,
  with no one passing through,
Now I will make you the pride of the ages,
  a joy from generation to generation.
¹⁶You shall suck the milk of nations,
  and be nursed at royal breasts;
And you shall know that I, the LORD, am
    your savior,
  your redeemer, the Mighty One of Jacob.
¹⁷Instead of bronze I will bring gold,
  instead of iron I will bring silver;
Instead of wood, bronze;
  instead of stones, iron.
I will appoint peace your governor,
  and justice your ruler.
¹⁸No longer shall violence be heard of in your
    land,
  or plunder and ruin within your borders.
You shall call your walls "Salvation"
  and your gates "Praise."

Eternal Light for Zion

¹⁹No longer shall the sun
  be your light by day,
Nor shall the brightness of the moon
  give you light by night;
Rather, the LORD will be your light forever,
  your God will be your glory.
²⁰No longer will your sun set,
  or your moon wane;
For the LORD will be your light forever,
  and the days of your grieving will be over.
²¹Your people will all be just;
  for all time they will possess the land;
They are the shoot that I planted,
  the work of my hands, that I might be
    glorified.

continue

be no more. The surviving nations, however, are clearly subordinate to Judah. They bring their wealth to Jerusalem and serve its people. What this text reflects is not universalism but religious nationalism.

Second, a critical element in the prophet's vision is his expectation that the people of Jerusalem will be just. This is the foundation of the new Jerusalem. Gone will be the social distinctions of the past, the economic oppression, and the political domination of the poor by the people of means. This new society will be God's doing. Of course, the prophet recognizes that this new society is a long way from being realized. It is not surprising that the book of Revelation uses this text to speak about the heavenly Jerusalem (60:3, 11, 19; Rev 21:23, 25-26).

In the return of the nations envisioned by the prophet (60:4-9), all **the children of Abraham** come to Jerusalem to worship the Lord: descendants of Isaac (Jews) from near and far, descendants of Abraham's wife Keturah from Midian and Sheba (Gen 25:2-4), descendants of Ishmael from Kedar and Nebaioth (Gen 25:25:13). Even the Gentiles, adopted children of Abraham (see Rom 4:11-12), come from Tarshish.

61:1-3 The prophet's mission

Isaiah describes his mission in terms of justice for the oppressed in language similar to 42:1-4, 49:1-6, and 50:4-11. While the "captives" are the people of Judah still in exile in Babylon, the prophet certainly sees his mission in broader terms. The "afflicted" and the "brokenhearted" in verse 1 are the victims of the corrupt and incompetent leadership that the prophet condemned in 56:9-12 and 58:1-9. Here he comes back to a significant Isaianic motif: justice for the poor. Judah is condemned to exile because of the injustice of its economic and social system. God will recreate Judahite society according to justice, and the prophet has a central role in the working out of God's plan.

> ²²The least one shall become a clan,
>   the smallest, a mighty nation;
> I, the LORD, will swiftly accomplish
>   these things when the time comes.
>
> ### CHAPTER 61
>
> #### The Anointed Bearer of Glad Tidings
>
> ¹The spirit of the Lord GOD is upon me,
>   because the LORD has anointed me;
> He has sent me to bring good news to the afflicted,
>   to bind up the brokenhearted,
> To proclaim liberty to the captives,
>   release to the prisoners,
> ²To announce a year of favor from the LORD
>   and a day of vindication by our God;
> To comfort all who mourn;
>   ³to place on those who mourn in Zion
>   a diadem instead of ashes,
> To give them oil of gladness instead of mourning,
>   a glorious mantle instead of a faint spirit.
>
> *continue*

"The spirit of the Lord GOD" is a characteristic Isaianic expression used to describe the presence and power of God in the world. The prophet uses this phrase to underscore his belief that Jerusalem's liberation and restoration are the work of God, not a human achievement. Jerusalem's future will not be determined by any king, Judahite or Persian. It will be the result of miraculous transformation of society. Though the prophet has a role in that transformation, he exercises that role only because of the anointing of God's Spirit on his life.

Luke has Jesus read this text during synagogue worship and then assert that it had been fulfilled in him (Luke 4:17-19). The evangelist reflects the early Christian belief that God's Spirit has been poured out upon Jesus in a unique way to accomplish the divine plan that

Restoration and Blessing

They will be called oaks of justice,
   the planting of the LORD to show his glory.
⁴They shall rebuild the ancient ruins,
   the former wastes they shall raise up
And restore the desolate cities,
   devastations of generation upon generation.
⁵Strangers shall stand ready to pasture your flocks,
   foreigners shall be your farmers and vinedressers.
⁶You yourselves shall be called "Priests of the LORD,"
   "Ministers of our God" you shall be called.
You shall eat the wealth of the nations
   and in their riches you will boast.
⁷Because their shame was twofold
   and disgrace was proclaimed their portion,
They will possess twofold in their own land;
   everlasting joy shall be theirs.

God's Word of Promise

⁸For I, the LORD, love justice,
   I hate robbery and wrongdoing;
I will faithfully give them their recompense,
   an everlasting covenant I will make with them.
⁹Their offspring shall be renowned among the nations,
   and their descendants in the midst of the peoples;
All who see them shall acknowledge them:
   "They are offspring the LORD has blessed."

Thanksgiving for God's Deliverance

¹⁰I will rejoice heartily in the LORD,
   my being exults in my God;

continue

---

will effect the salvation of Israel and the nations. Luke believes that the prophet's vision was fulfilled in Jesus—but fulfilled in a way that far exceeded the prophet's profoundest hopes and wildest expectations.

61:4-11 The priesthood of the poor

The prophet does not describe the political and religious institutions of the new Jerusalem in any detail as Ezekiel does. He prefers language that is more evocative than descriptive. For example, the prophet implies that in the new Jerusalem the role of the king will be taken by the people as a whole (55:3-5). Did this mean that the prophet did not envision the restoration of Judah's native dynasty? Here the prophet speaks to the people of the new Jerusalem and asserts that they "shall be called 'Priests of the LORD'" (61:6). Does this mean that he did not envision the restoration of the Zadokite priesthood, the descendants of Aaron and keepers of the temple, to its unique position in the new Jerusalem? What the prophet describes is the priestly role that the people of the new Jerusalem will play in regard to the nations. These "Priests" will lead the nations to serve Judah's God. The rebuilding of the temple and the renewal of priestly service do not appear to be priorities for the prophet. What is more significant for him is the renewal of Judahite society on the basis of justice. A just society brings with it God's blessing and is the embodiment of the covenant between God and Jerusalem.

The prophet understands his mission to Israel to be the creation of a just society, one that will be the envy of the whole world. God has anointed him, i.e., designated him solemnly to overcome the social problems that are keeping Judah from becoming the type of community that can enjoy all God's benefits. Once that new society is created, the people can proceed with the restoration of their villages and cities that were devastated by Judah's political, military, and economic collapse.

Judah can free itself from foreign domination by creating a new society without religious hierarchy and social status. All the people will be priests and all the people will have access to the wealth with which God has blessed Judah. This new society will turn Judah's oppressors into its servants. This new society will bring wealth to its entire people. This new society is precisely what God wants Judah to establish. God will make an everlasting covenant with that new, just community, not with people who are devouring themselves through internal societal conflicts.

The book of Revelation asserts that the members of the Christian community are priests serving their God, thus fulfilling the prophet's vision (61:6; Rev 1:6; 5:10). The Magnificat, Mary's song in Luke, is a collage of Old Testament text that begins with a paraphrase of verse 10 (Luke 1:46).

> For he has clothed me with garments of salvation,
> and wrapped me in a robe of justice,
> Like a bridegroom adorned with a diadem,
> as a bride adorns herself with her jewels.
> ¹¹As the earth brings forth its shoots,
> and a garden makes its seeds spring up,
> So will the Lord GOD make justice spring up,
> and praise before all the nations.

Lesson Five

EXPLORING LESSON FIVE

1. Some scholars believe that chapter 56 begins a section of Isaiah that reflects a later period in history, when the exiles have begun reoccupying Jerusalem. According to 56:1-8, what conduct was required upon returning to Jerusalem in order to be counted among God's people? (See 58:13-14; Wis 3:14.)

2. Isaiah shows no tolerance for Jerusalem's unjust and incompetent leaders in this period (56:9–57:13), telling them to rely on their idols when they are in trouble since they have not trusted in the one true God (57:13). How does idolatry still manage to distract us from relying on God? (See Col 3:5.)

3. a) What does the prophet describe as true fasting (58:6-10)? (See Zech 7:9-10; Ezek 18:5-9.) How would you explain this in your own words and experience?

   b) How does this lesson take shape in the New Testament? (See Mark 2:18-20; Matt 25:31-46; Acts 13:2-3; 14:23.)

Lesson Five

4. a) Why did Sabbath observance become so significant in the years following the exile (58:13-14)?

   b) Describe some ways that we can keep the Sabbath holy, without allowing such observances to become mere ritual (Mark 2:27).

5. In 59:1-8, the prophet describes the atmosphere after the return to Jerusalem. Why have old rivalries and divisions emerged so soon after the people's liberation from Babylon? (See Ezra 4:1-5; Neh 1:1-4.)

6. What is striking to you in the confession of sin found in 59:9-15 and God's response in 59:15-21? (See Neh 1:5-11.)

7. Isaiah 60:1-6 is proclaimed at Mass on the feast of the Epiphany. How does it apply to this feast? (See Ps 72:8-15; Matt 2:1-12.)

Lesson Five

8. Chapter 60 elaborately describes former enemies and other nations coming to Jerusalem. What is the apparent message in this context (60:14-16)? (See 61:5-7.)

9. a) To those who returned from exile and re-established themselves in Jerusalem, what is the message of 61:1-3?

   b) How do you understand these verses in your own life when you hear them on the lips of Jesus (Luke 4:18-19)?

10. In what sense will God's people be "Priests of the Lord" (61:6)? (See Exod 19:6; Rom 15:15-16.)

CLOSING PRAYER

Prayer

For thus says the high and lofty One,
 the One who dwells forever, whose name is
  holy:
I dwell in a high and holy place,
 but also with the contrite and lowly of
  spirit,
To revive the spirit of the lowly,
 to revive the heart of the crushed. (Isa 57:15)

Exalted God, you extend your mercy and saving grace to all of your children: rich and poor, foolish and wise, sinner and saint. We need only respond to the offer of your friendship to be admitted into the circle of your love. Inspire us to imitate your concern for us by our own acts of charity toward one another. We pray today especially for . . .

LESSON SIX

Isaiah 62–66

Begin your personal study and group discussion with a simple and sincere prayer such as:

Prayer

Lord God, as we continue our study of Isaiah, may our hearts remain open to the prophet's proclamation of your boundless love for your people. Inspire us with your Spirit so we may always be moved to seek you and to serve one another.

Read the Bible text of Isaiah 62–66 found in the outside columns of pages 92–101, highlighting what stands out to you.

Read the accompanying commentary to add to your understanding.

Respond to the questions on pages 102–104, Exploring Lesson Six.

The Closing Prayer on page 105 is for your personal use and may be used at the end of group discussion.

Lesson Six

CHAPTER 62

A New Name for Zion

¹For Zion's sake I will not be silent,
    for Jerusalem's sake I will not keep still,
Until her vindication shines forth like the dawn
    and her salvation like a burning torch.
²Nations shall behold your vindication,
    and all kings your glory;
You shall be called by a new name
    bestowed by the mouth of the LORD.
³You shall be a glorious crown in the hand of
    the LORD,
    a royal diadem in the hand of your God.
⁴No more shall you be called "Forsaken,"
    nor your land called "Desolate,"
But you shall be called "My Delight is in her,"
    and your land "Espoused."
For the LORD delights in you,
    and your land shall be espoused.
⁵For as a young man marries a virgin,
    your Builder shall marry you;
And as a bridegroom rejoices in his bride
    so shall your God rejoice in you.
⁶Upon your walls, Jerusalem,
    I have stationed sentinels;
By day and by night,
    they shall never be silent.
You who are to remind the LORD,
    take no rest,
⁷And give him no rest,
    until he re-establishes Jerusalem
And makes it the praise of the earth.

continue

and asserts that it will be Yahweh's queen. The city's reversal of fortunes will be marked by its new names: "My Delight" and "Espoused" (62:4). The prophet exploits the image of Jerusalem as a woman to speak about the city's coming restoration and glorification. God is being reconciled with Jerusalem as a husband is reconciled with his estranged wife. This union will bring fertility to the land and the rebuilding of the city.

 Renaming as a means of signifying a change in status or relationship is a well-known motif in the Bible (see Gen 17:3-5; 32:29; John 1:42; Acts 4:36). The change in Jerusalem's name from "Forsaken" (*Azubah*) or "Desolate" (*Shemamah*) to "My Delight is in her" (*Hepzibah*) and "Espoused" (*Beulah*) reflects a change in God's relationship to the now-vindicated city (62:4). These new names for Jerusalem have lived on in a variety of ways, including in popular literature. Nathaniel Hawthorne names the heroine of *The House of the Seven Gables* Hepzibah, while John Bunyan calls the pleasant country adjacent to the heavenly city "the land of Beulah" in his allegory *The Pilgrim's Progress*.

62:1-5 The new Jerusalem: The Lord's bride

The prophet recognizes that his vision of a new Jerusalem has not been realized. Instead of retracting or modifying his argument, he restates his points in a more forceful fashion. There will be a new Jerusalem for all peoples to see. Then using feminine grammatical forms for Jerusalem, the prophet addresses the city

In his description of Jerusalem as **"a glorious crown in the hand of the Lord"** (62:3), Isaiah may be echoing a common image in neighboring religions. The patron deities of various cities in the ancient Middle East were frequently depicted as holding the walls of their cities as crowns in their hands. There are also possible hints to the meaning of Isaiah's image in Jewish wedding customs of the time, where both bride and groom wore crowns. This latter association brings together three elements found in Isaiah 62:1-5 (a name change, a crown, and an explicit reference to marriage) that are all components of a traditional Jewish wedding.

62:6-12 Daughter Zion

The prophet calls upon the people of Jerusalem to remind the Lord of the promises made to Jerusalem. They are to be so intemperate in their pleading that God will have no rest from their petitions. He concludes this chapter by assuring "daughter Zion" that her salvation is coming. The prophet addressed these words to people who considered themselves heirs to the promises made about the restoration of Judah, the liberation of Jerusalem, and the reversal of the fortunes of the poor. Though the prophet's visions have not come to fulfillment, he refuses to abandon them. While Jerusalem and Judah were economically depressed and politically impotent, the prophet speaks of the city's splendor. While that splendor is yet to be revealed, it is coming. The prophet can see God coming; he can see the new Jerusalem.

63:1-6 The Lord, the warrior

It is hard to imagine a more stunning shift in mood than the one that occurs here. The prophet leaves behind the poignant image of a husband reconciling with his wife. In this passage, God is a warrior returning from the battlefield with his clothes soaked with the blood of the enemy. Edom and its capital Bozrah symbolize the forces pressuring Judah and

The Blessings of Salvation for God's People

⁸The Lord has sworn by his right hand
 and by his mighty arm:
No more will I give your grain
 as food to your enemies;
Nor shall foreigners drink the wine,
 for which you toiled.
⁹But those who harvest shall eat,
 and praise the Lord;
Those who gather shall drink
 in my holy courts.
¹⁰Pass through, pass through the gates,
 prepare a way for the people;
Build up, build up the highway, clear it of
  stones,
 raise up a standard over the nations.
¹¹The Lord has proclaimed
 to the ends of the earth:
Say to daughter Zion,
 "See, your savior comes!
See, his reward is with him,
 his recompense before him."
¹²They shall be called "The Holy People,"
 "The Redeemed of the Lord."
And you shall be called "Cared For,"
 "A City Not Forsaken."

CHAPTER 63

The Divine Warrior

¹Who is this that comes from Edom,
 in crimsoned garments, from Bozrah?
Who is this, glorious in his apparel,
 striding in the greatness of his strength?
"It is I, I who announce vindication,
 mighty to save."
²Why is your apparel red,
 and your garments like one who treads
  the wine press?
³"The wine press I have trodden alone,
 and from the peoples no one was with me.
I trod them in my anger,
 and trampled them down in my wrath;

continue

Their blood spurted on my garments,
    all my apparel I stained.
⁴For a day of vindication was in my heart,
    my year for redeeming had come.
⁵I looked about, but there was no one to help,
    I was appalled that there was no one to
        lend support;
So my own arm brought me victory
    and my own wrath lent me support.
⁶I trampled down the peoples in my anger,
    I made them drunk in my wrath,
    and I poured out their blood upon the
        ground."

Prayer for the Return of God's Favor

⁷The loving deeds of the LORD I will recall,
    the glorious acts of the LORD,
Because of all the LORD has done for us,
    the immense goodness to the house of
        Israel,
Which he has granted according to his mercy
    and his many loving deeds.
⁸He said: "They are indeed my people,
    children who are not disloyal."
So he became their savior
⁹in their every affliction.
It was not an envoy or a messenger,
    but his presence that saved them.
Because of his love and pity
    the LORD redeemed them,
Lifting them up and carrying them
    all the days of old.
¹⁰But they rebelled
    and grieved his holy spirit;
So he turned to become their enemy,
    and warred against them.

¹¹Then they remembered the days of old, of Moses,
his servant:

Where is the one who brought up out of the
    sea
    the shepherd of his flock?
Where is the one who placed in their midst
    his holy spirit,

continue

preventing the restoration from proceeding as the prophet envisioned it. But God is determined to restore Judah so that a new, just society can emerge there. God will not allow any interference. Any nation that stands in the way of Judah's restoration will be subject to God's judgment and swept aside. God will accomplish this without the help of anyone—least of all Judah itself which has yet to create the kind of society that God is making possible.

In speaking of the final battle with the powers of evil, the book of Revelation describes the coat of the rider on the white horse as "dipped in blood," implying that the prophet's words will find their fulfillment at the end of this age (63:1; Rev 19:13).

 In contemplating the depiction of **God as a warrior**, we should always keep in mind that the same God is God of both the Old and New Testaments. The trend of contrasting a harsh and violent Old Testament God with a gentle and loving New Testament God is inaccurate and inauthentic. Both testaments share many images of God, including father, king, shepherd, warrior, eagle, rock, light, shield, fortress, and water.

63:7–64:11 A lament

The prophet shifts moods again as he prays for the restoration of Jerusalem. The prophet adopts the lament form, which tries to move God to act by reminding God of acts on Israel's behalf in the past and then by describing the difficulties experienced by Zion.

The prophet begins by singing of God's actions for Judah. God has been faithful, loving, and good to Israel. The people of Israel are God's people, so God suffered when they suffered and God saved them when they were about to be extinguished. Despite this, Judah has still continued its path of self-destruction. God did not abandon Judah to its fate but acted toward it as God did toward the exodus gen-

> ¹²Who guided Moses by the hand,
>   with his glorious arm?
> Where is the one who divided the waters
>   before them—
>   winning for himself an everlasting
>   renown—
> ¹³Who guided them through the depths,
>   like horses in open country?
> ¹⁴As cattle going down into the valley,
>   they did not stumble.
> The spirit of the LORD guided them.
> Thus you led your people,
>   to make for yourself a glorious name.
> ¹⁵Look down from heaven and regard us
>   from your holy and glorious palace!
> Where is your zealous care and your might,
>   your surge of pity?
> Your mercy hold not back!
>   ¹⁶For you are our father.
> Were Abraham not to know us,
>   nor Israel to acknowledge us,
> You, LORD, are our father,
>   our redeemer you are named from of old.
> ¹⁷Why do you make us wander, LORD, from
>   your ways,
>   and harden our hearts so that we do not
>   fear you?
> Return for the sake of your servants,
>   the tribes of your heritage.
> ¹⁸Why have the wicked invaded your holy
>   place,
>   why have our enemies trampled your
>   sanctuary?
> ¹⁹Too long have we been like those you do
>   not rule,
>   on whom your name is not invoked.
> Oh, that you would rend the heavens and
>   come down,
>   with the mountains quaking before you,
>
> **CHAPTER 64**
>
> ¹As when brushwood is set ablaze,
>   or fire makes the water boil!
> Then your name would be made known to
>   your enemies
>   and the nations would tremble before you,
> ²While you worked awesome deeds we could
>   not hope for,
>   ³such as had not been heard of from of old.
> No ear has ever heard, no eye ever seen,
>   any God but you
>   working such deeds for those who wait
>   for him.
> ⁴Would that you might meet us doing right,
>   that we might be mindful of you in our
>   ways!
> Indeed, you are angry; we have sinned,
>   we have acted wickedly.
> ⁵We have all become like something unclean,
>   all our just deeds are like polluted rags;
> We have all withered like leaves,
>   and our crimes carry us away like the wind.
>
> *continue*

eration. That generation too failed to respond faithfully toward the marvelous deeds that God worked for them in freeing them from slavery in Egypt. They murmured in the wilderness. Still, God saved them through Moses. God saved them from themselves.

Just as Moses interceded for the freed but rebellious Hebrew slaves, so the prophet intercedes for the freed but rebellious exiles and their descendants. The prophet calls God the "father" of the Judahites because their ancient ancestors Abraham and Jacob will not acknowledge them. The prophet is mystified by his people's pattern of rebellion and asks God to be Judah's king by rebuilding the temple so that Judah can once again call on God's name in God's sanctuary. The prophet's cry that God "rend the heavens and come down" (63:19) asks God to take immediate and decisive action to establish the new Jerusalem.

Lesson Six

⁶There are none who call upon your name,
  none who rouse themselves to take hold
    of you;
For you have hidden your face from us
  and have delivered us up to our crimes.

A Final Plea

⁷Yet, Lord, you are our father;
  we are the clay and you our potter:
  we are all the work of your hand.
⁸Do not be so very angry, Lord,
  do not remember our crimes forever;
  look upon us, who are all your people!
⁹Your holy cities have become a
    wilderness;
  Zion has become wilderness, Jerusalem
    desolation!
¹⁰Our holy and glorious house
  in which our ancestors praised you
Has been burned with fire;
  all that was dear to us is laid waste.
¹¹Can you hold back, Lord, after all this?
  Can you remain silent, and afflict us so
    severely?

CHAPTER 65

¹I was ready to respond to those who did not ask,
  to be found by those who did not seek
    me.
I said: Here I am! Here I am!
  To a nation that did not invoke my name.
²I have stretched out my hands all day
  to a rebellious people,
Who walk in a way that is not good,
  following their own designs;
³A people who provoke me
  continually to my face,
Offering sacrifices in gardens
  and burning incense on bricks,
⁴Sitting in tombs
  and spending the night in caves,

continue

In chapter 64, the prophet continues his prayer on Judah's behalf, pleading that the people experience God's presence and power as their ancestors did long before. The prophet is confident because God saves those who are righteous. Still, the prophet's overwhelming fear is that Israel's infidelity and sin have the power to keep God from restoring Judah. Zion now experiences God's absence because of its infidelity.

The prophet uses all his skill to move God to compassion and forgiveness. The people are God's creation. Can God continue to ignore the fate of the chosen people? Jerusalem and its temple have been devastated. Can God continue to allow these to remain in ruins? God should not allow this terrible situation to continue. Forgiveness and restoration are what the prophet asks of God. In assessing the reasons for the failure of the restoration, the prophet does not find fault with God but with Judah (64:5), and so has the people confess their sins. Similar confessions became common in early Jewish prayer (e.g., Neh 9:1-37). Also, the prophet does not approach God as a righteous judge who must deal with Judah's sins, but as a father whose love for his erring children remains constant (63:16).

Jesus used this image of God frequently and the prayer that he taught his disciples addresses God as "our father" just as Isaiah's prayer does (see Matt 5:9). In speaking about the spiritual wisdom of the believer, Paul imitates the language of 64:3 (see 1 Cor 2:9).

65:1-16 God's response

The preceding prayer tried to move God to action, but, speaking in the name of God, the prophet affirms that God has always been ready to act. The Judahites themselves ignored their God. But they have done more than this. They have provoked God through aberrant religious practices including the violation of dietary laws that, along with sabbath observance and circumcision, became the marks of Jewish self-identity. By ignoring the dietary laws, some Judahites effectively placed themselves outside the Jewish community. There is only one pos-

Eating the flesh of pigs,
  with broth of unclean meat in their dishes;
⁵Crying out, "Hold back,
  do not come near me, lest I render you holy!"
These things are smoke in my nostrils,
  a fire that burns all the day.
⁶See, it stands written before me;
  I will not remain quiet until I have repaid in full
⁷Your crimes and the crimes of your ancestors as well,
  says the LORD.
Since they burned incense on the mountains,
  and insulted me on the hills,
I will at once pour out in full measure
  their recompense into their laps.

Fate of the Just and Unjust in Israel

⁸Thus says the LORD:
As when the juice is pressed from a cluster,
  and someone says, "Do not destroy it,
    for there is still good in it,"
So will I do for the sake of my servants:
  I will not destroy them all.
⁹From Jacob I will bring forth offspring,
  from Judah, those who are to possess my mountains;
My chosen ones shall possess the land,
  my servants shall dwell there.
¹⁰Sharon shall become a pasture for the flocks,
  the Valley of Achor a resting place for the cattle,
  for my people who have sought me.
¹¹But you who forsake the LORD,
  who forget my holy mountain,
Who spread a table for Fortune
  and fill cups of mixed wine for Destiny,
¹²You I will destine for the sword;
  you shall all bow down for slaughter;
Because I called and you did not answer,
  I spoke and you did not listen,
But did what is evil in my sight
  and things I do not delight in, you chose,
¹³therefore thus says the Lord GOD:
My servants shall eat,
  but you shall go hungry;
My servants shall drink,
  but you shall be thirsty;
My servants shall rejoice,
  but you shall be put to shame;
¹⁴My servants shall shout
  for joy of heart,
But you shall cry out for grief of heart,
  and howl for anguish of spirit.
¹⁵You will leave your name for a curse to my chosen ones
  when the Lord GOD slays you,
  and calls his servants by another name.
¹⁶Whoever invokes a blessing in the land
  shall bless by the God of truth;

continue

sible response: divine judgment. Judah experienced it in the past; it will experience it anew. But there are those in the community whom the prophet calls God's "servants." These will not experience judgment but the blessings of the land that will provide what is necessary for their survival, food, and drink.

The Judahites then will not have a single destiny. There are those who "walk in a way that is not good," and there are God's "servants." Each group will have its own destiny in accordance with its response to the God who freed the exiles of Zion. There are two ways: one leads to life and the other to death. The prophet reminds the wicked what they have to look forward to.

In verses 1-2, the prophet is speaking about God's intention to seek out those Jews who have given up their ancestral religion; Paul applies these verses to the Gentiles whom God has "sought out" through Paul's mission (Rom 10:20).

Lesson Six

Whoever takes an oath in the land
  shall swear by the God of truth;
For the hardships of the past shall be
    forgotten
  and hidden from my eyes.

A World Renewed

¹⁷See, I am creating new heavens
  and a new earth;
The former things shall not be remembered
  nor come to mind.
¹⁸Instead, shout for joy and be glad forever
  in what I am creating.
Indeed, I am creating Jerusalem to be a joy
  and its people to be a delight;
¹⁹I will rejoice in Jerusalem
  and exult in my people.
No longer shall the sound of weeping be
    heard there,
  or the sound of crying;
²⁰No longer shall there be in it
  an infant who lives but a few days,
  nor anyone who does not live a full
    lifetime;
One who dies at a hundred years shall be
    considered a youth,
  and one who falls short of a hundred shall
    be thought accursed.
²¹They shall build houses and live in them,
  they shall plant vineyards and eat their
    fruit;
²²They shall not build and others live there;
  they shall not plant and others eat.
As the years of a tree, so the years of my
    people;
  and my chosen ones shall long enjoy
    the work of their hands.
²³They shall not toil in vain,
  nor beget children for sudden
    destruction;
For they shall be a people blessed by the LORD
  and their descendants with them.
²⁴Before they call, I will answer;
  while they are yet speaking, I will hear.

continue

65:17-25 The new world

The Jerusalem that the prophet envisions is clearly not the city he lives in. It will be part of the new world that God is about to bring into existence. The prophet concluded that this world would not be the place of the ultimate triumph of God's justice. God will create a new world and, of course, a new Jerusalem. This is the first step in the direction of Revelation's "new Jerusalem, coming down out of heaven" (Rev 21:1-3). The new Jerusalem that the prophet expects will be a joy and a delight, not the feeble and forlorn city of this world.

 In describing the new world that God will ultimately create (65:17-25), Isaiah emphasizes that violence of any kind will have no place there. The **peaceful coexistence of the wolf and the lamb** is made possible by the fact that there will no longer be a division of creatures into predators and prey: "the lion shall eat hay like the ox" (65:25). Thus, the new Jerusalem will see the restoration of God's original intention that all creation be nourished solely by plant life (Gen 1:29). It was only after the great flood that God gave Noah and his descendants "[a]ny living creature that moves" as food to eat (Gen 9:3).

For the prophet, Jerusalem has become a symbol of the new world that God will bring into existence. It is a world in which there will be no infant mortality. People will live into old age. They will enjoy their homes and vineyards and their children will grow into honorable adulthood. God will answer their prayers before they finish making them. In short, this passage describes a perfect world where "[t]he wolf and the lamb shall pasture together" (65:25), the kind of world the lyrical text of Isaiah 11:6-9 imagines. The utopian visions of chapters 11 and 65 were born of the disappointments experienced by the people of Jerusalem at very difficult periods of their lives. The disappointment of the Jerusalem community made it possible for texts such as 2 Peter 3:13 to reinterpret the prophet's vision of the "new heavens / and a new earth" (65:17, see also Isa 66:22) as coming when Jesus returns.

66:1-6 Worship and justice

This text severs the fate of Jerusalem from that of the temple. Verses 1-6 are as negative a statement on temple worship as is found in the Bible. Together with 1:10-20 they frame the book of Isaiah and suggest that one goal of the final form of the book as a whole reflected a conflict within the early Jewish community. On one side were the priests who believed that the rituals of the temple were the guarantees of Israel's future. On the other side were those who believed that a just social and moral order was more significant than any ritual. Verse 5 is a clear reference to that conflict, and the following verse asserts that those for whom the temple is so important will hear the voice of the Lord who comes to redress the injustices done to the poor.

The imagery of verse 1 must have passed into Jewish religious speech since Jesus calls heaven God's "throne" and the earth God's "footstool" (Matt 5:35; 23:22). Stephen cites verses 1-2 to argue that the building of the temple by Solomon was a mistake (Acts 7:49-50).

None shall harm or destroy on all my holy mountain, says the LORD.

²⁵The wolf and the lamb shall pasture together,
 and the lion shall eat hay like the ox—
 but the serpent's food shall be dust.
None shall harm or destroy
 on all my holy mountain, says the LORD.

CHAPTER 66

True and False Worship

¹Thus says the LORD:
The heavens are my throne,
 the earth, my footstool.
What house can you build for me?
 Where is the place of my rest?
²My hand made all these things
 when all of them came to be—oracle of the LORD.
This is the one whom I approve:
 the afflicted one, crushed in spirit,
 who trembles at my word.
³The one slaughtering an ox, striking a man,
 sacrificing a lamb, breaking a dog's neck,
Making an offering of pig's blood,
 burning incense, honoring an idol—
These have chosen their own ways,
 and taken pleasure in their own abominations.
⁴I in turn will choose affliction for them
 and bring upon them what they fear.
Because when I called, no one answered,
 when I spoke, no one listened.
Because they did what was evil in my sight,
 and things I do not delight in they chose,
⁵Hear the word of the LORD,
 you who tremble at his word!
Your kin who hate you
 and cast you out because of my name say,
"May the LORD show his glory,
 that we may see your joy";
 but they shall be put to shame.
⁶A voice roaring from the city,
 a voice from the temple;
The voice of the LORD
 rendering recompense to his enemies!

continue

Blessings of Prosperity and Consolation

⁷Before she is in labor,
  she gives birth;
Before her pangs come upon her,
  she delivers a male child.
⁸Who ever heard of such a thing,
  or who ever saw the like?
Can a land be brought forth in one day,
  or a nation be born in a single moment?
Yet Zion was scarcely in labor
  when she bore her children.
⁹Shall I bring a mother to the point of birth,
  and yet not let her child be born? says the Lord.
Or shall I who bring to birth
  yet close her womb? says your God.
¹⁰Rejoice with Jerusalem and be glad because of her,
  all you who love her;
Rejoice with her in her joy,
  all you who mourn over her—
¹¹So that you may nurse and be satisfied
  from her consoling breast;
That you may drink with delight
  at her abundant breasts!
¹²For thus says the Lord:
I will spread prosperity over her like a river,
  like an overflowing torrent,
  the wealth of nations.
You shall nurse, carried in her arms,
  cradled upon her knees;
¹³As a mother comforts her child,
  so I will comfort you;
  in Jerusalem you shall find your comfort.
¹⁴You will see and your heart shall exult,
  and your bodies shall flourish like the grass;
The Lord's power shall be revealed to his servants,
  but to his enemies, his wrath.
¹⁵For see, the Lord will come in fire,
  his chariots like the stormwind;
To wreak his anger in burning rage
  and his rebuke in fiery flames.
¹⁶For with fire the Lord shall enter into judgment,
  and, with his sword, against all flesh;
Those slain by the Lord shall be many.

continue

 Second and Third Isaiah (chapters 40–66) are characterized by many **feminine images**, referring both to God and the people:

Passage	Subject	Image
42:14	God	Woman in labor
45:10-11	God	Mother giving birth
47:1-15	Babylon	Dishonored woman, widow
49:15	God	Mother with infant
49:18-21	Zion	Bride, bereaved mother
50:1	Zion	Divorced wife
51:17-23	Jerusalem	Dishonored, bereaved mother
54:1-17	Zion	Restored wife and mother
61:10-11; 62:5	Zion	Bride
66:7-13	Zion	Mother giving birth and nursing

66:7-17 Jerusalem, our mother

Once Jerusalem is free from those who look to ritual as support for their injustice, Jerusalem will be able to fulfill its destiny as a mother to all believers. After God's judgment has purged the guilty, Jerusalem will give birth miraculously to many children "in a single moment" (66:8). The picture of "mother Zion" surrounded by her children is followed by another announcement of judgment on those who have perverted temple worship. Here the prophet concludes the transformation of Jerusalem from the woman who "was dismissed" (50:1) by her husband to the woman reunited with him and becoming a mother to his children.

66:18-24 The pilgrimage of the nations

The book of Isaiah ends with a familiar Isaianic theme: the pilgrimage of the nations to Jerusalem. They will join Israel in worship at "the house of the LORD," where new priests and Levites will replace those who have been purged because of their venality. This is a part of the new world that God is creating to effect the restoration of Israel—a restoration that will include all humanity except those who have rebelled. Jesus uses the imagery of verse 24 to speak about the punishment of those who lead others into sin (Mark 9:48).

The book ends on a negative note as it speaks about the fate of those who rebel against God. In rabbinic tradition, the public reading of the book of Isaiah concludes with the repetition of verse 23 to leave the hearers on a note of promise, not judgment.

> [17] Those who sanctify and purify themselves to go into the gardens, following one who stands within, eating pig's flesh, abominable things, and mice, shall all together come to an end, with their deeds and purposes—oracle of the LORD.
>
> #### God Gathers the Nations
>
> [18] I am coming to gather all nations and tongues; they shall come and see my glory. [19] I will place a sign among them; from them I will send survivors to the nations: to Tarshish, Put and Lud, Mosoch, Tubal and Javan, to the distant coastlands which have never heard of my fame, or seen my glory; and they shall proclaim my glory among the nations. [20] They shall bring all your kin from all the nations as an offering to the LORD, on horses and in chariots, in carts, upon mules and dromedaries, to Jerusalem, my holy mountain, says the LORD, just as the Israelites bring their grain offering in a clean vessel to the house of the LORD. [21] Some of these I will take as priests and Levites, says the LORD.
>
> [22] Just as the new heavens and the new earth
>   which I am making
> Shall endure before me—oracle of the LORD—
>   so shall your descendants and your name
>   endure.
> [23] From new moon to new moon,
>   and from sabbath to sabbath,
> All flesh shall come to worship
>   before me, says the LORD.
> [24] They shall go out and see the corpses
>   of the people who rebelled against me;
> For their worm shall not die,
>   their fire shall not be extinguished;
>   and they shall be an abhorrence to all flesh.

Lesson Six

EXPLORING LESSON SIX

1. In Scripture, what is the significance of receiving a new name from God (62:2-4, 12)? (See Gen 17:3-5; 32:29; John 1:42; Acts 4:36.)

2. What is the significance of the description of God coming from the direction of Edom as a bloody warrior (63:1-6)? (See 34:5-6; Ezek 25:12-13; Obad 12-14.)

3. In recalling God's deeds on Israel's behalf, the prophet emphasizes that God's very presence is the source of salvation (63:9). When you review your life thus far, in what ways have you become more aware of this gift of God's presence?

4. What does it mean in your spiritual life to "wait" for the Lord (64:3)? (See Ps 27:13-14; 40:2; 69:7; Rom 8:18-19.)

Lesson Six

5. a) What prevented Israel from recognizing God's presence and readiness to act on their behalf (65:1)?

b) What sometimes prevents you from this same awareness?

6. Throughout chapter 65, what phrases or descriptions are used to identify those who respond faithfully to God?

7. a) The tension between the value of temple worship versus the value of living justly (66:1-6) is never fully resolved. How does the same concern surface in the incident surrounding the martyrdom of Stephen in Acts 6:8-15 and 7:39-60?

b) What does Jesus say about the relative values of ritual worship and just living? (See Matt 9:13; 12:7.)

Lesson Six

8. In what ways might (or should!) God's word cause us to tremble in response (66:2, 5)? (See 1 Chr 16:29-30.)

9. In 66:7-13, Jerusalem and God are both depicted as a mother. How do such images help or challenge your ideas about God? (See 49:15; Ps 131:2; Matt 23:37.)

10. If you were asked to briefly describe a central message of the book of Isaiah, what would you say? What message, image, or passage from this great prophetic work resonates with you most?

CLOSING PRAYER

Prayer

> Yet, LORD, you are our father;
> we are the clay and you our potter:
> we are all the work of your hand. (Isa 64:7)

Lord our God, just as shapeless clay in the hand of the potter becomes a beautiful and useful vessel, so too does your Spirit move to make us our best and brightest selves. With joy we place ourselves in your hands. Shape us as you will, that we may be vessels of your love in this world. As our time of study draws to a close, we pray for one another, especially . . .

PRAYING WITH YOUR GROUP

Because we know that the Bible allows us to hear God's voice, prayer provides the context for our study and sharing. By speaking and listening to God and each other, the discussion often grows to more deeply bond us to one another and to God.

At *the beginning and end of each lesson* simple prayers are provided for individual use, and also may be used within the group setting. Most of the closing prayers provided with each lesson relate directly to a theme from that lesson and encourage you to pray together for people and events in your local community.

Of course, there are many ways to center ourselves in God's presence as we gather together in groups around the word of God. We provide some additional suggestions here knowing you and your group will make prayer a priority as part of your gathering. These are simply alternative ways to pray if your group would like to try something different from those prayers provided in the previous pages.

Conversational Prayer

This form of prayer allows for the group members to pray in their own words in a way that is not intimidating. The group leader begins with Step One, inviting all to focus on the presence of Christ among them. After a few moments of quiet, the group leader invites anyone in the group to voice a prayer or two of thanksgiving; once that is complete, then anyone who has personal intentions may pray in their own words for their needs; finally, the group prays for the needs of others.

A suggested process:
In your own words, speak simple and short prayers to allow time for others to add their voices.

Focus on one "step" at a time, not worrying about praying for everything in your mental list at once.

Step One	Visualize Christ. Welcome him. Imagine him present with you in your group. Allow time for some silence.
Step Two	Gratitude opens our hearts. Use simple words such as, "Thank you, Lord, for . . ."
Step Three	Pray for your own needs knowing that others will pray with you. Be specific and honest. Use "I" and "me" language.

Step Four   Pray for others by name, with love.
              You may voice your agreement ("Yes, Lord").
              End with gratitude for sharing concerns.

Praying Like Ignatius

St. Ignatius Loyola, whose life and ministry are the foundation of the Jesuit community, invites us to enter into Scripture texts in order to experience the scenes, especially scenes of the gospels or other narrative parts of Scripture. Simply put, this is a method of creatively imagining the scene, viewing it from the inside, and asking God to meet you there. Most often, this is a personal form of prayer, but in a group setting, some of its elements can be helpful if you allow time for this process.

A suggested process:

- Select a scene from the chapters in the particular lesson.
- Read that scene out loud in the group, followed by some quiet time.
- Ask group members to place themselves in the scene (as a character, or as an onlooker) so that they can imagine the emotions, responses, and thinking that may have taken place. Notice the details and the tone, and imagine the interaction with the Lord that is taking place.
- Share with the group any insights that came to you in this quiet imagining.
- Allow each person in the group to thank God for some insight and to pray about some request that may have surfaced.

Sacred Reading (or Lectio Divina)

This method of prayer invites us to "listen with the ear of the heart" as St. Benedict's rule would say. We listen to the words and the phrasing, asking God to speak to our innermost being. Again, this method of prayer is most often used in an individual setting but may also be used in an adapted way within a group.

A suggested process:

- Select a scene from the chapters in the particular lesson.
- Read the scene out loud in the group, perhaps two times.
- Ask group members to ponder a word or phrase that stands out to them.
- The group members could then simply speak the word or phrase as a kind of litany of what was meaningful for your group.
- Allow time for more silence to ponder the words that were heard, asking God to reveal to you what message you are meant to hear, how God is speaking to you.
- Follow up with spoken intentions at the close of this group time.

REFLECTING ON SCRIPTURE

Reading Scripture is an opportunity not simply to learn new information but to listen to God who loves you. Pray that the same Holy Spirit who guided the formation of Scripture will inspire you to correctly understand what you read, and empower you to make what you read a part of your life.

The inspired word of God contains layers of meaning. As you make your way through passages of Scripture, whether studying a book of the Bible or focusing on a biblical theme, you may find it helpful to ask yourself these four questions:

What does the Scripture passage say?
Read the passage slowly and reflectively. Become familiar with it. If the passage you are reading is a narrative, carefully observe the characters and the plot. Use your imagination to picture the scene or enter into it.

What does the Scripture passage mean?
Read the footnotes in your Bible and the commentary provided to help you understand what the sacred writers intended and what God wants to communicate by means of their words.

What does the Scripture passage mean to me?
Meditate on the passage. God's word is living and powerful. What is God saying to you? How does the Scripture passage apply to your life today?

What am I going to do about it?
Try to discover how God may be challenging you in this passage. An encounter with God contains a challenge to know God's will and follow it more closely in daily life. Ask the Holy Spirit to inspire not only your mind but your life with this living word.